In Search of Health and Wealth

In Search of Health and Wealth
The Prosperity Gospel in African, Reformed Perspective

Edited by
Hermen Kroesbergen

A Special Edition of the *Word and Context* Journal
Justo Mwale Theological University College, Lusaka, Zambia

WIPF & STOCK · Eugene, Oregon

IN SEARCH OF HEALTH AND WEALTH
The Prosperity Gospel in African, Reformed Perspective

Copyright © 2014 Wipf and Stock Publishers. All rights reserved. Except for brief quotations in critical publications or reviews, no part of this book may be reproduced in any manner without prior written permission from the publisher. Write: Permissions. Wipf and Stock Publishers, 199 W. 8th Ave., Suite 3, Eugene, OR 97401.

Cover photograph by Johanneke Kroesbergen-Kamps

Wipf & Stock
An Imprint of Wipf and Stock Publishers
199 W. 8th Ave., Suite 3
Eugene, OR 97401

www.wipfandstock.com

ISBN 13: 978-1-62564-141-0

Manufactured in the U.S.A.

Dedicated to
the memory of
Rev. F. D. Sakala
(1934–2012)
and
Rev. L. Z. B. Mwale
(1931–2012)

Contents

Introduction | ix
—Hermen Kroesbergen

Part 1: Background Examination

1. The Challenges of the Prosperity Gospel for Reformed/Presbyterian Churches in the Twenty-First Century | 3
—Victor Chilenje

Part 2: Biblical Analysis

2. "Fipelwa na baYaweh": A Critical Examination of Prosperity Theology in the Old Testament from a Zambian Perspective | 21
—Edwin Zulu

3. Is the Prosperity Gospel Biblical? A Critique in Light of Literary Context and Union with Christ | 29
—Dustin W. Ellington

Part 3: Theological Reflection

4. Jesus the Healer | 49
—Devison Telen Banda

5. Dialoguing at "Mphala": A Conversation on Faith between John Calvin and Proponents of the Prosperity Gospel | 59
—Lameck Banda

6. The Prosperity Gospel: A Way to Reclaim Dignity? | 74
—Hermen Kroesbergen

Part 4: Cultural Analysis

7 "Zambia Dziko la Chonde" | 87
—Lukas Soko

8 Dreams and Nightmares of Modernity: Accusations and Testimonies of Satanism in Zambia | 97
—Johanneke Kroesbergen-Kamps

9 African Gospreneurship: Assessing the Possible Contribution of the Gospel of Prosperity to Entrepreneurship in Light of Jesus's Teaching on Earthly Possessions | 110
—Lovemore Togarasei

List of Authors | 127

Introduction

THE PROSPERITY GOSPEL IS very influential in Africa, in Pentecostal churches and in Reformed churches as well. But what is the prosperity gospel? Where did it originate? Is it biblically sound? How should we evaluate the prosperity gospel? Does it represent a wrong way of looking for health and wealth, or can we learn something from it? In this book the authors provide an analysis from different perspectives on the highly debated topic of the prosperity gospel. It is intended to be accessible and helpful both to academic colleagues and to ordinary ministers. Most of the authors are lecturers at Justo Mwale Theological University College in Lusaka, Zambia. Together with Prof. Lovemore Togarasei from the University of Botswana, they use their theological skills to examine and assess this important topic from an African and Reformed perspective. The articles in this book will help anyone who wants to deeply explore and evaluate the intriguing phenomenon of the prosperity gospel in Africa.

In the first part of the book a background examination of the prosperity gospel is provided. Here Victor Chilenje discusses the historical and missiological background of the phenomenon. The main teachings are outlined, as are the attraction of and the problems with the prosperity gospel. This is followed by a second part which presents a biblical analysis of the prosperity gospel. Edwin Zulu investigates the roots of the phenomenon in the Old Testament. In a critical examination he shows the ways in which the prosperity gospel can and cannot be said to be based on Old Testament teachings. The use of the New Testament in the prosperity gospel is analyzed by Dustin Ellington. First, Ellington challenges all sides of the prosperity gospel debate to go beyond hurling biblical proof texts back and forth at each other. Second, he illustrates his argument, critiquing the message of

Introduction

prosperity by addressing its neglect of one of the New Testaments most prevalent themes: union with Christ.

Whereas the first part of this book looks at the historical background and the second part provides a biblical analysis of the prosperity gospel, the third part provides a theological reflection on the prosperity gospel. The issue of health is dealt with by investigating Jesus as Healer within an African context. The arrival of the prosperity gospel has challenged mainline churches to address the issue of health more seriously. Devison Telen Banda, in his article, provides the basis for an African Christology that pays due attention to the importance of health, especially in Africa. The African context is addressed by Lameck Banda as well. He uses the local African concept of "mphala" to mediate between the idea of faith in the prosperity gospel and in the work of John Calvin. "Mphala" is an encompassing concept which refers to a space for social networking. As such it may very well serve as a foundational concept, particularly in the Africa context, toward building bridges between the prosperity gospel and mainline churches from the Reformed tradition. After the theological treatment of the themes of health and faith, Hermen Kroesbergen theologically discusses the idea of prospering, using the work of Søren Kierkegaard. He investigates both what is eccentric and what is valuable in the prosperity gospel. He concludes by proposing a litmus test to distinguish a genuine prosperity gospel from theologically unacceptable forms of it.

A cultural analysis of the prosperity gospel is provided in the fourth and final part of this book. Lukas Soko investigates its relationship to the rise of mass media, using Zambia as an example. The prosperity gospel's importance is connected to the ability of its adherents to use globalised mass media. Soko urges churches to take seriously the challenges of globalization and accept the prosperity gospel as a given reality. Discernment is needed, so he concludes. A different type of discernment is addressed in the next article. Johanneke Kroesbergen-Kamps discusses the intriguing link between modernity and Christianity in the Zambian context by analyzing the confession of a former Satanist. Is it a coincidence, she asks, that especially in churches with an emphasis on prosperity, testimonies of involvement in Satanism are quite popular? Kroesbergen-Kamps places these testimonies in the context of the search for modernity, health and wealth. Lovemore Togarasei introduces the term "gospreneurship" to highlight the close connection between prosperity teachings on God and on entrepreneurship. In light of Jesus's teaching on earthly possessions

Introduction

Togarasei assesses the possible contribution of the prosperity gospel to entrepreneurship. With this article discussing the relevance and biblical soundness of the prosperity gospel, in the African context of entrepreneurship as a means of poverty alleviation, our volume, *In Search of Health and Wealth*, ends on a hopeful note.

This book mainly resulted from discussions we had on the prosperity gospel theme at Justo Mwale Theological University College in 2012. Academically, educationally and personally, 2012 was a good year for our institution; this book is intended to share some of the institutions accomplishments. However, there was sad news as well. In 2012 Justo Mwale Theological University College lost two of its former principals. On 12 June Rev. F. D. Sakala passed away. His life was honored at a very well-attended service in the Anglican Cathedral. Ten days later his friend and colleague Rev. L. Z. B. Mwale died as well. May they rest in peace. We will always remember these two heroes who helped make JMTUC what it is today. This book is dedicated to the memory of these two high-regarded former principals as a tribute to their major contributions to the institution, the church and society at large.

To conclude, I want to express my gratitude to Sherri Ellington and Johanneke Kroesbergen-Kamps for the many hours they spent editing and proofreading the text of this book, and to Edwin Zulu, Rector of Justo Mwale Theological University College, and CLF, the publisher of the African edition for their contributions to make this book possible.

Hermen Kroesbergen

PART 1

Background Examination

1

The Challenges of the Prosperity Gospel for Reformed/Presbyterian Churches in the Twenty-First Century

VICTOR CHILENJE

THE PROSPERITY GOSPEL POSES many challenges for Reformed/Presbyterian churches in the twenty-first century. I will discuss the historical and missiological background of the phenomenon, using both secondary literature and oral interviews to illustrate the prosperity gospel with first hand experiences. The main teachings are outlined, as well as the attraction and the problems of the prosperity gospel.

"Prosperity" is generally defined as a prosperous condition, material wellbeing and success (Webster 1998:1013). "Gospel" is the story that brings good news about Jesus as our Lord and Savior of the whole world (Webster 1998:545). The challenge of the prosperity gospel is that people are attracted to its message of wealth and health, and do not recognize that the message is not biblical. Because of the attraction of the prosperity gospel message many Reformed church members, especially in urban areas, have dual membership. In the morning they attend worship services in their established Reformed/Presbyterian churches, but in the afternoon they go to churches where they feel they may receive health and wealth (Mwanza 2012; Kachali 2012). When told to "sow a seed" (this is a concept that pastors use when raising money in their congregations and ministries)

Part 1: BACKGROUND EXAMINATION

they do not hesitate to contribute financially to the prosperity congregation because they believe by doing so they will receive blessings from God.

The prosperity gospel may also be called the Word-Faith movement. It is frequently also called word of faith, the faith movement, or name-it-and-claim-it. It is the belief that Christians have, within themselves, the supernatural power to create reality by speaking a word (Walker 2007:347). This faith movement gives hope to the people, mostly the marginalised or hopeless.

The prosperity gospel poses a big challenge to Reformed/Presbyterian churches in the twenty-first century, a challenge so enormous that it requires attention by the entire church. The prosperity gospel has crept into the Reformed/Presbyterian churches, and the results are increasingly distorted biblical principles—a terrifying development which must be addressed. Proponents of the prosperity gospel preach physical well-being that is measured by the amount of wealth an individual has. This includes good food, clothing, vehicles and houses. It should be noted that how someone acquires the wealth does not matter; people are normally told to believe that all the blessings are received by faith. Issues of health and wealth are also promised by these proponents of the prosperity gospel (Sakala 2012).

When the prosperity gospel creeps into Reformed/Presbyterian churches, a second result is conflict—between minister and Presbytery/Synod leadership, minister and congregational members, and/or within the church membership. Conflict arises between minister and Presbytery/Synod leadership when the leadership assigns a pastor to a poor rural congregation. The rural congregation is unable to support the pastor at the level of prosperity gospel pastors seen first-hand in urban areas or on television. The rural pastor resents the Church leadership for "punishing" him by assigning him to a rural congregation.

Conflict arises between minister and congregants when the minister disparages the small contributions poor congregants contribute as tithe and offering. The minister may encourage the congregants to go see how members of a large Pentecostal church care for or "bless" their pastor.

Conflict arises between members of the congregation—especially between elderly and youth—because of their different understandings of the biblical message. Older members are likely to reject the prosperity gospel while youth will often consider it.

The Church in Africa is at a cross roads, not knowing how to choose between the teachings of the Reformed churches and the wealth and material blessings promised by the prosperity gospel as a sign of the faithfulness and righteousness of the recipients. The sad truth is that in Africa health and wealth are not equitably distributed in the church and the society. People found in impoverished urban and rural areas are attracted to the prosperity gospel message they hear on television or other media or during visits to churches. However, prosperity gospel pastors, seeking health and wealth as promised by proponents of the prosperity gospel, refuse to preach in poor areas because people do not have the resources to "sow a seed." Mainline church congregants, harangued by pastors to give beyond their means, feel the God being worshipped in the church is the God of the rich, not a God who cares for the poor (Chilembo 2012; Chunda 2012). For church members in typical rural areas, living in abject poverty, without support from government services or non-governmental organizations, hoping only in holistic Christian ministries, the prosperity gospel is pure nonsense. It contradicts the Bible. It is meaningless—only sand.

Historical Overview of the Prosperity Gospel

The origin of the prosperity gospel movement can be traced to the United States of America in the early twentieth century. The founder of the prosperity gospel "faith movement" was Mr. Essek William Kenyon (1867–1948), a pastor and founder of Bethel Bible Institute. Mr. Kenyon was an ordained Methodist minister. He left the Methodist church and founded several churches which he linked to the Baptist church. It should be noted that Mr. Kenyon cherished and maintained good relationships with the pioneers of the Pentecostal movements in the United States of America and leaders on other continents (Walker 2007:252, 347). However, he never accepted all their teachings and doctrines.

Subsequently, he came in touch with the ideas and teachings of the "New Thought" which was founded by Phineas Parkhurst in 1838. Parkhurst taught that the mind has the ability to heal the body (Walker 2007:237).

The Christian Science movement, founded by Mary Baker Eddy, also influenced Mr. Kenyon as he started the prosperity gospel movement. Eddy taught that sin, sickness and death are illusions and thus can be cured through right thinking (Walker 2007:100; Martin 2003:149–55).

Kenyon wrote that Christians could make a "positive confession" to bring emotional and physical desires into being. He stated, "What I confess, I possess" (Phiri and Maxwell 2007). As the Pentecostal pastor and scholar

Part 1: BACKGROUND EXAMINATION

J. Norberto Saracco from Argentina explains in his informative entry on "Prosperity theology" in the *Dictionary of Mission Theology*, Kenyon believed that the spread of his teaching about the power of the human mind to overcome sin and sickness would result in human beings who would not be affected by evil spirits or by illness or poverty (Saracco 2007:323).

Kenyon in turn influenced the Pentecostal beliefs of Mr. Kenneth Hagin (1917–2003). He added Kenyon's teaching to his own to create what would become the Word-Faith movement. As an Assemblies of God pastor, Mr. Hagin taught Christians they could get rich if they had enough faith. He preached that words spoken in faith, related to health and wealth, must be fulfilled because God is required to honor the words. Hagin urged his believers to "say it, do it, receive it, tell it" (Walker 2007:323; Phiri and Maxwell 2007). Many within the movement recognize Kenneth Hagin as one of the fathers of the movement, even referring to him as Dad Hagin.

It was Mr. Kenneth Copeland (1936–present) who helped to restructure and organize the prosperity gospel movement. A young associate of Oral Roberts, Copeland began teaching in the 1960s that faith is a "force" which brings material results when confessed out loud. Within a couple of decades, Word-Faith grew into a significant offshoot of charismatic faith (Walker 2007:90, 347–48).

Other popular word-faith teachers include Kenneth Hagin Jr, Gloria Copeland, Charles Capps, Creflo Dollar, Frederick K. C. Price, Paul and Jan Crouch, Casey Treat, Marilyn Hickey, Jesse Duplantis and Earl Paulk (Walker 2007:348).

How did the prosperity gospel find its way to Africa? Pentecostalism opened the door in the early 1900s. As a result of the 1906 Azusa Street Revival in Los Angeles, ordinary but "called" people fanned out to every corner of the globe as missionaries. They were untrained and inexperienced; their only qualification was baptism in the Spirit and a divine call. Through their efforts to win souls to Christ, Pentecostalism was planted throughout Africa, and became an integral part of African Initiated Churches (AICs) (Walker 2007:252–53; Mullin 2008:211–12).

In the early 1990s Kenneth Hagin, his son Kenneth Hagin Jr, and Kenneth Copeland visited AICs across Nigeria preaching the prosperity gospel. The impact was immense. Churches after that grew into millions of members, and the gospel of wealth found its way into the heart of Africa's church. For example, in a 2006 Pew survey, 85 percent of Kenyan Pentecostals, 90 percent of South African Pentecostals and 95 percent of Nigerian

Pentecostals indicated that God grants prosperity to all believers who have enough faith. In addition about nine out of ten Kenyan, Nigerian and South African Pentecostals said religious faith is very important to economic success. And, according to Allan H. Anderson, professor of Global Pentecostal Studies at the University of Birmingham, "older (denominational) churches are struggling to keep up with the jet-setting entrepreneurs who head up these new (Pentecostal) organizations" (Phiri and Maxwell 2007).

The rise of television evangelism also contributed greatly to the spread and impact of the prosperity gospel. Prosperity gospel teachers embraced televangelism during the 1960s, and grew to dominate American religious programming (Chunda 2012).

As Africans acquired television sets, viewers watched American programming, and African prosperity gospel teachers developed their own shows which were watched by millions of viewers across Africa (Mphande 2012).

The Main Teachings of the Prosperity Gospel

Sowing a Seed

The main teachings of the prosperity gospel are that faith results in health and wealth, that God wants his people to be blessed by security and prosperity, and that sickness and poverty are curses to be broken by faith. The doctrine teaches that faith, positive speech and donations to Christian ministries will increase one's material wealth (Hood 2004:57–65; Kachali 2012).

Prosperity gospel proponents teach that poverty is a curse (Deut 28:1). They state that God blesses those who live upright and keep his covenant. It is added that Jesus said: "According to your faith will it be done to you" (Matt 9:29). Psalm 112:3 supports this view by stating that: "Wealth and riches are in his house, and his righteousness endures for ever." Ecclesiastes 5:19 is quoted as follows: "When God gives any man wealth and possessions, and enables him to enjoy them, to accept his lot and be happy in his work—this is a gift of God."

Another verse prosperity gospel proponents very much quote is Joshua 1:7–8, which states that if you follow God you will receive blessings when going out and coming in. The prosperity gospel teaches that the Bible says: "For no matter how many promises God has made, they are 'Yes' in

Christ. And so through him the 'Amen' is spoken by us to the glory of God" (2 Cor 1:20). The prosperity gospel adds that "God did not create poverty, but it came as a result of the fall of man" (Gen 3:1). It is not his will for his people to continue living in poverty. Furthermore, prosperity gospel proponents use verses such Luke 6:38; Galatians 6:7; and 2 Corinthians 9:6–8 to justify their teaching that, as a Christian, you need to tithe, give to the poor, and promote the gospel with your money to receive God's financial blessings (Rouse 1999:115–17).

Prosperity gospel members are taught that when you give a financial contribution, you "plant a seed" which will multiply and return to you in abundance. In the same vein, prosperity gospel proponents teach that "you plough back," a phrase again meaning the donation multiplies and returns to the giver. The proponents emphasize that giving "gives an identity to God," a phrase used to indicate that by giving financially God will recognize you as his faithful child (Sakala 2012).

The Law of Sowing and Reaping

The prosperity teaching interprets Mark 10:29–30 in the sense that we will receive from God a hundred times what we put into his hands. The main exponents of prosperity theology emphasize that "whoever puts into practice this law would practically enter into a cycle of endless wealth" (Saracco 2007:323).

The believers' faith itself (independent of God's direct action or will) contains financial prosperity. Those who believe this tend to also believe it is a spiritual law that applies to both the believer and the nonbeliever (Walker 2007:337–38). Faith in the concept is fundamental, regardless of whether or not the individual believes in God. It is the faith itself that "creates" financial blessing.

Proclaiming and Having

In today's global village the emphasis is on positive thoughts. In social media people most often write about the good things that happened to them, including issues concerning their health and wealth. Prosperity theology has been reinforced by this emphasis on positive thought. This theology focuses on being pragmatic or practical, meaning belief is required in order to achieve tangible results and concrete benefits in the material world. The power of positive thinking is encouraged in all members of their church so they can benefit from the results. It is strongly stated that "your belief will help create the fact." Positive thought attracts riches, success, health and happiness (Saracco 2007:323; Sakala 2012).

Saracco (2007:324) clearly explains the prosperity gospel's interpretation of

> *the law of the proclaimed word.* The formula is "proclaim to have." Hagin said, "You can have what you say" (*Having Faith in Your Faith*). The text which is most used to back this idea is Mark 11:23–24. According to this interpretation, the force of faith is released by words. It is not sufficient to believe something in the heart, but for something to become real, it is necessary to confess it.

A believer needs to confess out loud what he wants to have. This implies that when we confess something negative it will become a reality and the positive the same. Therefore we live according to what we say (Mwanza 2012).

Believers are little gods or divine beings who possess all or some of the distinctive attributes of God. As little God's, believers can therefore emulate God, who spoke all things into existence. This means words are containers of power. Whatever one speaks will occur, be it negative or positive. Therefore one should only speak positive or faith-filled words (Walker 2007:337–8). Members are taught that positive thought and a positive verbal declaration create health and wealth, while a negative attitude and declaration lead to poverty and illness (Sakala 2012; Chilembo 2012).

The Power of Blessing

Many exponents of this faith movement agree that the power to secure wealth comes from God. They base their belief on their interpretation of specific scriptures. For example, Deuteronomy 8:18 speaks of God's covenant with his people: "But remember the Lord your God, for it is he who gives you the ability to produce wealth, and so confirms his covenant, which he swore to your forefathers." And Psalm 105:37 says, "He brought out Israel, laden with silver and gold, and from among their tribes no-one faltered." The Bible confirms this in Matthew 6:33: "But seek first his kingdom and his righteousness, and all these things will be given to you as well." Psalm 35:27 affirms: "The Lord be exalted, who delights in the well-being of his servant." Furthermore, exponents of the faith movement believe that the word of God brings blessings to his people so that they can enjoy them. "The blessing of the Lord brings wealth, and he adds no trouble to it" (Prov 10:22). And in Psalm 1:1–3 we find: "Blessed is the man who does not walk in the council of the wicked or stand in the way of sinners or sit in the seat of mockers. But his delight is in the law of the Lord, and on his law he meditates day and night. He is like a tree planted by streams of water, which yields its fruit in season and whose leaf does not wither. Whatever he does prospers."

This law of blessing is based on God's covenant with Abraham. Prosperity theologians claim that the main reason God made the covenant with Abraham was to bless him materially. Therefore Christians, as spiritual sons of Abraham, are heirs of the blessings of the covenant. In view of this, Christians must affirm that prosperity is God's will because he wants us to prosper in all areas of life. This includes possessing the best homes, the best cars, the best clothes. These are the inheritance of the faithful servants of God (Saracco 2007:323).

The Work of Christ

The prosperity gospel movement believes both in divine healing and in material prosperity through Jesus Christ's redeeming work on the cross. They teach that in Christ's death, resurrection and ascension, God put our sins, illness, and poverty on Him so that we may be able to enjoy the blessings of our salvation (Walker 2007:337–8).

The Attraction of the Prosperity Gospel

The teachings of the prosperity gospel movement churches have attracted many adherents in Africa and elsewhere. These adherents believe that for religion to be meaningful, it must be practical, dynamic, and problem-solving. It should be noted that, despite negative criticism, these churches are attracting many members (Kubi and Torres 1981:120).

While many Reformed/Presbyterian churches are reported to be declining in membership, income, and staff in today's world, the prosperity gospel movement/church is the fastest growing body of Christian believers worldwide. Membership in Pentecostal and charismatic churches in Africa has risen from seventeen million in 1970 to 147 million in 2005 (Phiri and Maxwell 2007).

The prosperity gospel movement offers tremendous promise to the 315 million sub-Saharan Africans living on less than a dollar a day. For them, teaching about the cross and about suffering may be unappealing. The promise of prosperity is hard to resist. The prosperity gospel is attractive to those from Reformed traditions who have been taught blessing must wait until the next life (Sakala 2012; Mwanza 2012).

The prosperity gospel has incorporated many elements of the Reformed churches, and Reformed churches have incorporated some elements of prosperity gospel. As a result, worship in prosperity gospel churches is familiar to Christians from the mission churches (Chunda 2012; Mwanza 2012). However, worship services in the prosperity gospel movement churches also incorporate many elements of traditional African culture. These include oral liturgy, narrative theology and witness, and recounting visions and dreams. Their worship services are characterized by reconciliatory and participatory worship, liturgical dance and prayers of healing and exorcism, which are predominant African cultural features (Anderson 2000).

People are also attracted to the prosperity gospel because it reflects the traditional African concept of blessedness. In the African context, blessedness is understood in terms of the biological and material, not just the religious/spiritual aspects. Africans have always considered land, children, animals, good health and good harvest all as wealth and blessing from the Supreme Being (Mugambi and Wasike 1992:60).

In addition, traditional African thought acknowledges that man has to solicit spiritual help to protect and enrich his/her physical life. Prosperity gospel adherents do not hesitate to ask for physical riches and prosperity, which in a sense become a measure of favor or blessings from God and the departed. Africans traditionally also share their prosperity with God and the departed through sacrifices, thanksgiving, and other acts of remembrance (Mbiti 1975:56–57). These ideas resonate with the prosperity gospel.

The prosperity gospel attracts people from all social classes. It appeals to those who have possibilities of advancement in life, such as business men and women, public sector employees, and those employed with international non-governmental organizations. With emphasis on wealth, health and blessings, it promotes belief and expectation of economic and social progress among the lower middle classes. It attracts persons from

Part 1: BACKGROUND EXAMINATION

the higher middle classes who wish to increase their resources. Persons from impoverished lower classes, who tend to go to faith movements that emphasize divine healing or miracles, appreciate the emphasis on health. Some persons from the higher classes, who prefer experience with mystical emphases, are drawn to the overall theology (Saracco 2007:325). Wealthy people, who are able to "sow substantial seeds," appreciate being held in high esteem by the prosperity gospel pastor, and are happy to claim their wealth as a blessing from God (Mwanza 2012).

This movement also meets the psychological needs of the people. Members of these congregations are divided into small groups where they are trained in prosperity gospel beliefs. They learn that, for a financial contribution, they can submit a prayer request to the pastor, and he will pray for them. Some detractors from the prosperity gospel movement would say that it is the idea that the pastor is praying for the individual's specific concern that provides the individual with psychological relief (Mwanza 2012).

The prosperity gospel leaders preach blessings to people, and who does not desire wealth and healing? For example, in Nigeria, Rev. Felix Omobude promises crowds that "women will find husbands, audience members will buy new cars, and the barren will birth twins" (Phiri and Maxwell 2007).

At the same time, people want supernatural healing powers that counteract the forces of evil, diseases, and witchcraft, to mention but a few. The prosperity gospel churches offer spiritual and supernatural protection to members through their spiritual leaders (Kachali 2012). In addition, University of Calgary professor Irving Hexham suggests that the prosperity gospel fulfils the African desire for communication with the supernatural through visions and dreams. South African members speak of the wonderful dreams of Kenneth Hagin's communication with God—understood by prosperity gospel proponents as the result of "sowing a seed." Intellectual faith pales in comparison to a Christian faith described by prosperity teachers as a lifestyle of direct communication with God (Phiri and Maxwell 2007).

People perceived as rich, powerful leaders—from the local village headman to the paramount chief to the nation's president—are honoured and respected in Africa (Mphande 2012). These categories of persons are known as "Big Men" in Africa. Churches in which the prosperity gospel is taught are usually directed by a sole pastor or strong leader who commands authority similar to the traditional African chief and headmen. Pastors like

Michael Okonkwo, bishop of the Redeemed Evangelical Mission based in Nigeria, are the "Big Men" in modern day Africa, adorned with all the trappings of a successful tribal chief. They attract huge followings because of their wealth, power and showmanship (Phiri and Maxwell 2007).

Problems of Prosperity Gospel Teachings

The prosperity gospel is at best half truth. Saracco (2007:324) shows this very clearly:

> Passages such as Mark 10:30, 11:22 and 11:23–24 are key to the prosperity gospel, and interpreted by forcing their [the prosperity movement's] arguments on the translation. For example, the hundredfold reward promised by Jesus in Mark 10:30 is not a formula for personal enrichment but a show of God's love toward those who have left all for his cause. Even so, the same passage clarifies explicitly that these blessings will not preclude adversity.

In the Bible the emphasis is always on faith, and not on the audible expression of what we want to achieve. The words do not have power in themselves—it is God in his sovereignty who decides to bless us or withhold material blessings for now.

God does bless us, but it should also be noted that the so-called spiritual laws or principles which preach immediate and concrete blessing lack support from the scriptures. Blessings come because of the grace of God and God's sovereignty (Saracco 2007:324). According to biblical teachings found, for example, in stories of Abraham and Joseph, perseverance and patient waiting, perhaps for generations, are required for the blessing to be obtained (Kachali 2012).

To be blessed is to be granted special favor by God with resulting joy and prosperity. In the Old Testament there was considerable emphasis on material blessing; however in the New Testament, the emphasis is on spiritual blessing. Jesus Christ bore the consequences of the curse for believers (Gal 3:13) and blessed them with the forgiveness of sins (Rom 4:6). As a result of receiving God's blessings in Christ, believers are called to be a source of blessing to the world, especially in response to those who persecute them (Luke 6:27–28; Rom 12:14; 1 Cor 4:12; 1 Pet 3:9).

In some instances, prosperity gospel preachers take advantage of persons with limited education, few financial resources, and even intellectual disability. They sometimes visit lower income villages and towns where

Part 1: BACKGROUND EXAMINATION

they induce persons limited in their understanding of the word of God to give almost everything they have to the church for the sake of receiving material blessings from God. People have given money, farms, houses, even their retirement package to the prosperity gospel preacher, who then leaves the community. The promised blessings do not materialize so the individuals end up destitute—without food, clothing or shelter (Kachali 2012). In addition, the situation of the now-destitute person is blamed on their lack of faith and they become outcasts (Sakala 2012; Chunda 2012). The prosperity gospel can be used to take advantage of the poor, on the one hand, or to encourage greed and selfishness in others. Its approach is a scandal when it emphasizes material rather than spiritual blessings, portraying Christ as the God of riches; neglecting Christian values of humility, sacrificial love, and commitment which characterize the kingdom of God; and emphasizing that proper relationship with God must be seen in physical as well as spiritual blessings (Saracco 2007:326; Mwanza 2012). The focus on storing up treasures on earth as a primary goal of faithful living is completely at odds with orthodox Christianity, which speaks of spiritual treasure stored in heaven (Falsani 2009).

People are attracted to the prosperity gospel because its emphasis on material blessing is comforting and easy. However, it ignores the role of suffering and sacrifice to which Christ calls his followers, and which he modeled for them. It ignores the blessings which are received through suffering (Gen 37:1; 38:1; 39:1; 40:1; 41:1; 42–47). It ignores that even when we are not receiving material blessings, God is there, watching and waiting for us to trust him, obey him, and learn that in loving him we have life's deepest blessing (McKnight 2009).

The prosperity gospel teaches that health and healing are also attached to giving—that is, "sowing a seed." The person seeking healing must donate financially to the church before and after healing prayer is offered (Kachali 2012).

In contrast to the above distortion of the gospel, the Bible has much to say about healing and health from a holistic perspective, totally divorced from monetary considerations. The Bible considers healthful living from the physical, the spiritual and the psychological standpoints (Mphande 2012). The physical strength and well-being of the body is never despised or dismissed, but is aptly summarized by the apostle's prayer: "Dear friend, I pray that you may enjoy good health and that all may go well with you, even as your soul is getting along well," or "prospereth" as the KJV translation reads (3 Jn 1:2). The concept of health includes all areas of the individual's existence—body, mind, and spirit—as the psalmist suggests: "Why are you downcast, O my soul?" (Ps 42:11).

Forgiveness and cleansing from sin will bring health and healing (Jer 30:12–17; 33:6–8). The redemptive work of Christ is the greatest healing force known to man, for guilt, bitterness, hatred, envy and other negative attitudes are removed, which are in themselves sickness, and which in turn cause all manner of mental and physical illness.

The prosperity gospel has already crept into the Reformed/Presbyterian churches, where ministers and members preach: "Give to brother and give to sister so that you can receive the blessings of God." This is done in the name of stewardship and is an abuse of the tithe. The tithes in these prosperity gospel churches go to a few individuals, while widows, widowers, orphans and vulnerable children are not considered (Kachali 2012; Mwanza 2012).

The prosperity gospel has brought greed into the church of God. In anyone's vocabulary, this is a nasty word; greed is "an illness of the soul." Greed is a sin that few of us confess and one that we rarely notice in our own behaviour (Hood 2004:49). In addition, greed is self-sufficient and self-centred (Tongoi 2001:32). Ministers in wealthy congregations are unwilling to share their surplus to support God's ministry in congregations where members are unable to raise stipends for their ministers. Instead the greedy minister challenges his poor colleague to "sow a seed and receive blessings from God." The greedy attitude of prosperity gospel ministers has resulted in instances of division and hatred between poorer and wealthier congregations and pastors (Stott 1996: 148; Mwanza 2012; Chunda 2012).

Generally speaking, prosperity gospel churches do not offer a holistic ministry which addresses, for example, literacy, clean water, education, and agriculture in the local community. As a result, the prosperity gospel perspective is viewed by many Presbyterian church members in Zambia as anti-development. Prosperity gospel ministers focus on personal wealth and not on the spiritual and physical development of congregations and communities. They are not interested in improving quality of life for communities. What matters to these ministers is their own welfare (Mwanza 2012; Kachali 2012).

In addition, most churches in the prosperity movement are nondenominational and independent, and the pastor is the highest organizational authority. The idea that a pastor should be accountable to members or elders is rejected. This leaves the congregation open to all sorts of abuse by the pastor, as he/she has no one to limit power and actions. The congregations are also open to heresy and theological error (Stott 1996:148; Chunda 2012).

The Way Forward

It should be recognized that always Christians must remember that the greatest wealth any one can have is not financial, but is a relationship with Jesus, the son of God (Rouse 1999:118).

Theological institutions need to make clear to their students the fallacies of the prosperity gospel. A component addressing problems of the prosperity gospel should be incorporated into all courses, from Old Testament 1, to Systematic Theology, to Theology of Ministry—even courses in Hebrew and Greek, where students can be asked to study the original understanding of prosperity and shalom.

Concerns with the prosperity gospel and how it impacts lives of individuals must also be addressed in small groups dealing with spiritual formation at theological institutions. This should include looking at how maturity in Jesus Christ can be lived out, and even deepened, through persisting in love during times of pain, betrayal and difficulty.

Proper exegesis and interpretation of the word of God must be emphasized. This is the primary tool which can help students and theologians avoid misinterpretation of God's word (Tate 2000: xix–xxvi).

Pastors who have received proper grounding in their theological institutions must be encouraged to address the misconceptions of the prosperity gospel in their congregations through studies and discussions at all levels and in all groups including the Women's Guild, Men's Guild, Christian Youth Fellowship, section studies, and from the pulpit. Teaching must be incorporated into conferences conducted at Presbytery and Synod levels.

Conclusion

This article focused on discussing the challenges of the prosperity gospel for Reformed/Presbyterian churches in twenty-first century Africa. The research, conducted in literature, internet and oral sources, identified real challenges that need to be addressed. These are:

- Widespread acceptance of emphasis on materialism preached by prosperity gospel pastors. Reformed/Presbyterian church members need to be firmly grounded in Reformed theology so they recognize misinterpretation.
- Division between members, ministers and congregations because of greed, envy of wealth and disagreement about theology and doctrine. Reformed/Presbyterian pastors and members need to receive spiritual formation that lifts up Reformed theology, especially that pain and suffering is part of Christian life.
- Abuse of, rather than concern for, the poor. Jesus's ministry of liberation and transformation in rural Palestine among marginalized people must be emphasized as a model for modern day preachers and teachers.
- Focus on personal gain rather than holistic ministry. Jesus's holistic ministry of healing, teaching, and praying among the poor, widows and children must be emphasized as a model of maturity in Jesus Christ.

Following this research and discussion, it is apparent that the prosperity gospel has made strong inroads into the theology of Reformed/ Presbyterian churches in Africa.

It has also been revealed that a way forward is needed which has to be holistic in its approach, to combat the fallacies of the prosperity gospel and to enhance the development of the church of God to its full potential.

Bibliography

Literature

Anderson, A. 2000. "The Pentecostal Gospel, Religion and Culture in African Perspective." [online] Available at: Artsweb.bham.ac.uk/aanderson/publications/pentecostal_gospel.htm.

Falsani, C. 2009. "The Worst Ideas of the Decade: The Prosperity Gospel." *Washington Post* [online]. Available at: http://www.washingtonpost.com/wpsrv/special/opinions/outlook/worst-ideas/prosperity-gospel.html.

Hood, N. 2004. *God's Wealth: Whose Money Is it Anyway?* Carlisle: Paternoster.

Kubi, K. A., and S. Torres. 1981. *African Theology en Route*. New York: Orbis.

Martin, W. 2003. *The Kingdom of the Cults*. Minneapolis: Bethany House.

Mbiti, J. S. 1975. *The Prayers of African Religion*. New York: Orbis.

Part 1: BACKGROUND EXAMINATION

McKnight, S. 2009. "The Problem for the Prosperity Gospel." Beliefnet.com [online]. Available at: http://www.beliefnet.com/Faiths/Christianity/2009/03/The-Problem-for-the-Prosperity-Gospel.aspx?p=1.

Mugambi, J. N. K., and A. Nasimiyu-Wasike, A., eds. 1992. *Moral and Ethical Issues in African Christianity: Exploratory Essays in Moral Theology*. Nairobi: Initiatives.

Mullin, R. B. 2008. *A Short World History of Christianity*. Louisville: Westminster John Knox.

Phiri, I., and J. Maxwell. 2007. "Gospel Riches: Africa's Rapid Embrace of Prosperity Pentecostalism Provokes Concern—and Hope." *Christianity Today* [online]. Available at: www.christianitytoday.com/ct/channel/utilities/print.html?type=article&id=46571.

Rouse, T. 1999. *Faith and the Pharisees: Sincere Critics Have Been Sincerely Wrong about the Word of Faith Teaching*. Yale: Insight.

Saracco, J. N. 2007. "Prosperity Theology." In J. Corrie, ed., *Dictionary of Mission Theology: Evangelical Foundations*. Nottingham: Inter-Varsity Press.

Stott, J. 1996. *Guard the Truth: The Message of 1 Timothy and Titus*. Downers Grove, IL: InterVarsity Press.

Tate, W. R. 1991. *Biblical Interpretation: An Integrated Approach*. Rev. ed. Peabody, MA: Hendrickson.

———. 1997. *Biblical Interpretation: An Integrated Approach*. Peabody: Hendrickson.

Tongoi, D. O. 2001. *Mixing God with Money: Strategies for Living in an Uncertain Economy*. Nairobi: New Life Literature.

Walker, J. K. 2007. *The Concise Guide to Today's Religions and Spirituality*. Eugene: Harvest House.

Webster, 1998. *The New International Webster's Comprehensive Dictionary of the English Language*. Naples, FL: Trident International.

Oral Sources

Chilembo, Z. 2012. "Interview about Prosperity Gospel." Interviewed by Dr. V. Chilenje [oral interview]. Lusaka, 11 September 2012.

Chunda, C. 2012. "Interview about Prosperity Gospel." Interviewed by Dr. V. Chilenje [oral interview]. Lusaka, 28 August 2012.

Kachali, J. 2012. "Interview about Prosperity Gospel." Interviewed by Dr. V. Chilenje [oral interview]. Lusaka, 28 August 2012.

Mwanza, T. 2012. "Interview about Prosperity Gospel." Interviewed by Dr. V. Chilenje [oral interview]. Lusaka, 27 August 2012.

Sakala, H. 2012. "Interview about Prosperity Gospel." Interviewed by Dr. V. Chilenje [oral interview]. Lusaka, 13 September 2012.

Mphande, P. 2012. "Interview about Prosperity Gospel." Interviewed by Dr. V. Chilenje [oral interview]. Lundazi, 11 October 2012.

PART 2

Biblical Analysis

2

"Fipelwa na baYaweh"[1]

A Critical Examination of Prosperity Theology in the Old Testament from a Zambian Perspective

EDWIN ZULU

THE ADVENT OF TELE-PREACHERS in Zambia and the growth of Pentecostal churches have changed perceptions about prosperity[2] in our country, and there is a steady following of prosperity theology. The teaching (prosperity theology) often asserts that being a Christian is a guarantee of good life and material wealth. In addition, there is also the assertion that this life needs to be free from suffering or sickness as these are not the will of God, and, by implication, whoever is suffering can be deemed to be living in sin.

---

1. This is a popular *Bemba* (Zambian Language) expression that means riches are given by God and it is mostly used in chorus, stickers and posters in many churches, particularly Pentecostal denominations.

2. The term *prosperity* is a relative term and it can be applied in different ways depending on the context. In this chapter the term will refer to the assumed blessing bestowed on people by God. The term came into being in the twentieth century, though some scholars urge that the notion that to gain something is godly can be traced to the time of Job.

Part 2: BIBLICAL ANALYSIS

However, we contend in this paper that, while it is an undisputed fact that God blesses his own people to prosperity in a broad sense, there is need to critically analyze prosperity in a holistic manner so that the physical and spiritual dimensions of prosperity are adequately addressed.

Old Testament Perspective on Prosperity: An Overview

General View of Prosperity Theology

The issue of prosperity theology has been discussed from various vantage points by various people. However, what is clear is that prosperity in the Old Testament is provided by God. It is God that makes one prosper and it is a gift from God (Deut 8:18). There are many passages that attest to that fact in the entire Old Testament. For example: "The blessing of the Lord brings wealth, and he adds no trouble to it" (Prov 10:22). Or: "Moreover, when God gives any man wealth and possessions, and enables him to enjoy them, to accept his lot and be happy in his work—this is a gift of God" (Eccl 5:19).

We agree with Prof. Andrew E. Hill's (1986:1012) view that there ought to be a strong emphasis on the importance of both the spiritual and ethical dimensions of prosperity. This means that we cannot overemphasize the ethical side of prosperity by stressing the alleged dubious reputation of wealthy people and the moral dangers of wealth, as many people do. Prosperity in the Old Testament was also further linked to the covenant (Deut 28:29; 29:9). In short, "it is God who bestows prosperity on those who keep and do the words of the Mosaic . . . covenants" (Hill 1986:1012).

It needs to be pointed out that we share the view that prosperity envisaged in the Old Testament denotes a number of things. According to Hill (1986:1012) it ranges from the realization of one's goals (Gen 24:21,40,42,56); to success in labor (Gen 39:3,23); to living in peace (*shalom*), safety (Deut 23:6, 1 Chr 14:7), and happiness (Lam 3:17); to enjoying the benefits of familial relationships (Ruth 4:11, Job 1:1–5); to acquiring and possessing material goods (Deut 28:11, 1 Kgs 10:7, 1 Chr 29:23, Job 21:33).

Prosperity and Suffering

The Old Testament also linked prosperity to suffering. The question often being asked is whether prosperity entails the absence of suffering. However, examining the Wisdom literature, for example, it is clear that prosperity cannot be the absence of suffering. One can prosper but still suffer, for example, as can be deduced from the life of Job.

We are therefore in agreement with C. E. Green (2010:128), who summarizes thus: "God is certainly a God of prosperity but definitely not a God of consumerist values and materialism. The materialistic orientation of the prosperity gospel means that the triumphs, glory and honor of the cross are emphasized to the neglect of its representation of pain and suffering. If triumph is always assured, it becomes nearly impossible to handle failure, defeat and suffering."

Therefore, we cannot rule out suffering even in our pursuit for prosperity. God still remains our refuge even in the time of trouble (Ps 9:9).

Prosperity and Righteousness

In the Old Testament prosperity is also linked to righteousness. We can see this in texts like: "The blessing of the Lord brings wealth, and he adds no trouble to it" (Prov 10:22), "Misfortune pursues the sinner, but prosperity is the reward of the righteous. A good man leaves an inheritance for his children's children, but a sinner's wealth is stored up for the righteous" (Prov 13:21–22), and "His children will be mighty in the land; the generation of the upright will be blessed" (Ps 112:3). Therefore, one cannot steal in the name of prosperity. This is so because, as T. Rouse says (1999:115), "God blessed those who lived right, did His will, and believed in His covenant."

Prosperity and Hard Work

In most discussion on the matter it is overlooked that there is some kind of "work ethic" attached to prosperity. While it is true that God is the one who blesses, it is also important that one works hard to attain wealth and to meet all physical needs. This is reflected in texts like: "Lazy hands make a man poor, but diligent hands bring wealth" (Prov 10:4), and "He who loves pleasure will become poor; whoever loves wine and oil will never be rich" (Prov 21:17).

Part 2: BIBLICAL ANALYSIS

Zambian Perspective on Prosperity: An Overview

General View

It is a commonly known fact that most people in Africa, and specifically in Zambia, live in poverty. This means that they lack basic needs such as basic shelter, education, health and water. The level of poverty creates in many the desire to move out of their situations, and consequently the people in this situation are vulnerable to any efforts that promise them relief. This explains why they would take any program with promises that comes their way, even programs that may con them.

The advent of tele-preachers in Zambia and the growth of Pentecostal churches have changed perceptions about prosperity in our country. Most of these preachers have been preaching a "gospel" that promises prosperity to those who accept it as a reward, so to speak. God gives, and everyone that has accepted God must be able to experience some kind of prosperity. In most instances this prosperity is measured by physical wealth, which is displayed through nice designer clothing, expensive motor vehicles, and good houses, just to mention a few examples. Furthermore, the means of obtaining these material gains is not important; in most cases, what matters is what one has got. These "riches" are given by God, usually as some kind of reward or compensation for good deeds and behavior.

It needs to be stated that what is significant in this regard is the absence of attention to suffering and righteousness in this prosperity. For example, one may have five wives with a number of children one cannot afford to take care of; this would be still be considered prosperity. In addition, one can acquire wealth by any means, even through witchcraft practices; what matters is what one gets. In this regard, the means does not matter, but the end.

Even stealing would be an acceptable means to attain prosperity. There is a common African saying which urges that: stealing is when one takes too much for himself." In other words, if one takes little for himself/herself, one has not stolen, even if he/she took something that does not belong to him or her.

However, as Zambian Christians we cannot condone this kind of mentality as it undermines honesty and hard work. By stealing one would be denying others a chance to benefit in terms of development. The resources stolen may have been meant to benefit a community and not an individual.

Mainline Churches' View of Prosperity

The matter of prosperity has been discussed at various levels in the mainline churches. However, from the onset we need to state that the matter is highly debatable. There usually two sides: one in full support of prosperity theology, and one made up of those who reject the teaching as not in line with biblical teachings. The critical side may be attributed to some historical factors related to the establishment of these churches. Most of these churches were established by missionaries who mainly propagated a gospel of humility and living a simple life. In most instances the emphasis was on piety as a response to the gospel. In some instances there has been an overemphasis on spirituality, whereby wealth, or the pursuit of it, was considered to be an earthly-motivated factor and therefore not in tandem with Christian virtues. Consequently a "sojourner" mentality or motif was created, in that Christians considered their stay on earth as temporal. This is evidenced in hymns that are still common today such as: "This world is not my home, I'm just passing through. My treasures (riches) are laid up somewhere beyond the blue (heaven)" (*Hymns for Malawi*, no. 371).

However, we need to state that, over the years, there has been a shift from the sojourner motif to a more balanced view of prosperity. There is a great appreciation that it is God who gives prosperity and people have to acknowledge it as a gift. In addition, there is a growing realisation that prosperity also demands righteousness; therefore, the way one obtains wealth comes to the fore. This means that wealth needs to be properly acquired.

We need to point out, also, that wealth cannot be expected to arrive on a silver platter; it also demands hard work. People need to work hard to acquire wealth, as work is considered spiritual (Job 7:1–2).

The Old Testament views prosperity in a holistic manner. This is the stance taken up by most mainline churches. Prosperity cannot be associated only with physical material gains, but may entail a number of things (see above). In other words, prosperity entails both spiritual and physical dimensions. It cannot be merely one of the two aspects.

In addition, we need to state that prosperity is not absence of suffering. There have been assertions that to be poor or suffering means you are not prosperous. In our relationship with God we might experience suffering and want, but that does not mean we are not blessed.

Part 2: BIBLICAL ANALYSIS

Pentecostal Churches' View of Prosperity

According to A. Burrick (2009), "Pentecostal churches are largely associated with the teaching (of prosperity). In a 2006 Pew Forum survey, a majority of Pentecostals in the 10 countries surveyed said they believed God would grant good health and relief from sickness to believers who had enough faith. In nine of countries, most Pentecostals say that God will grant material prosperity to all who have enough faith. Higher majorities of African believers were found to embrace the teachings."

The premise of discussions in most Pentecostal churches is that God gives prosperity to those that are in relationship with Him. If one accepts the LORD, the consequence is blessings. This is so because God always wants his people to prosper. As quoted before, in Proverbs we read: "The blessing of the Lord brings wealth, and he adds no trouble to it" (Prov 10:22). Therefore, prosperity is measured by physical and visible riches. The message of God is the means to come out of one's dire situation. One just needs to pray and fast; God will pour out his blessings. In other words, one just needs to claim the blessings because one is entitled to them by virtue of becoming a believer (Christian). The common saying is: "God has played his part; you just need to play your part, as well, by claiming the blessing."

The most controversial fact is that you need to do something for yourself to get it, i.e., plant a seed and the seed will grow. While it is understandable that one needs to do something about one's situation, it is not correct to assert that if one is in a dire situation it means one is not doing something about it or one is sinful. Placing the blessings in the hands of humans to some extent implies that humans can manipulate God. In addition, by asserting that as human beings we can determine our blessings, we place humans at the centre and leave out God. Furthermore, it is also not correct to assert that everyone who believes in God must be abundantly blessed physically. To be blessed entails a holistic prosperity that could be spiritual as well as physical. God cannot solve all our financial problems when we become Christians, but he can provide possibilities for us through which we can deal with our various problems.

In view of the above, belief in God (Jesus) is not a sure guarantee for material, financial, and health gains. Furthermore, money or wealth cannot be a symbol of a good life. There are many people with wealth who are living a horrible life without peace, always looking behind their backs to see if someone will come to take what they have.

African-Initiated Churches' View on Prosperity

Zambia has a lot of African-Initiated Churches with various teachings on prosperity. However, a view often projected is that riches are for this world: we should not desire things from this world but from the next. As members of the Zionist church would say: "We are going to heaven." This perspective helps explain why most of these churches are found in poor areas or in villages, where people are in vulnerable situations. It gives them hope to believe a message that one day they will leave this earth and go to live in a land of plenty.

In most instances, members of these churches point out that riches lead to sin, and that, consequently, rich people will not inherit heaven. For this reason, they urge that the soul is what needs to be rich.

Conclusions

The argument can be summed up as follows:
- Firstly, prosperity is linked to God's provision. It is a gift from God.
- Secondly, prosperity is linked to righteousness and suffering.
- Thirdly, prosperity is attained by hard work.
- Fourthly, prosperity is not only associated with physical and material gains. It denotes a number of things; it is more than material gains.

We need to state that it is not a disputed fact that God blesses his own people with prosperity. However, what is in dispute is a theology that places prosperity under the control of humans, as if humans can manipulate God into giving them prosperity, and a theology that measures prosperity only by material wealth. This kind of theology is misplaced and not in full agreement with biblical teaching. Riches are given by God freely—as we are used to saying in Zambia "Fipelwa na baYaweh"—and prosperity involves more than just material wealth. A theology of prosperity that does not recognize the blessings God can bestow on his followers is misplaced and alienated from reality. Therefore, the Church needs to teach a theology of prosperity that acknowledges God and his righteousness, but also is accepting of suffering.

A holistic view of prosperity in the Zambian context could help people in the extreme poverty levels to start to view themselves positively and

Part 2: BIBLICAL ANALYSIS

work towards liberating themselves from these demeaning situations. This is true despite some pathologies often associated with prosperity theology.

For this reason, we agree with T. Rouse (1999:211) that, "contrary to what the critic says, the prosperity message does not teach a lifestyle of self-indulgence and selfishness, but rather obedience and faith."

Lastly, people need not to feel guilty of their wealth if it is honestly acquired. In fact the Bible gives us a number of examples of godly people who were prosperous and it was God who made them prosper in their lives (Gen 13:2; 24:1; 26:12–13; Jer 32:42). Therefore, we cannot totally reject prosperity theology as pathology. It can contribute to poverty reduction, to self reliance, to self-worth, to dignity and to motivation to succeed.

Bibliography

Birch, B. C., W. Brueggemann, T. Fretheim, and D. L. A. Petersen. 2005. *Theological Introduction to the Old Testament*. 2nd ed. Nashville: Abingdon Press.

Burrick, A. 2009. "Prosperity Gospel Teachings 'Distort' Bible, Says Lausanne Group." *Christianity Today* [online]. Available at: http://www.christiantoday.com/articledir/print.htm?id=24926.

Eller, V. 1973. *The Simple Life: The Christian Stance toward Possessions*. Grand Rapids, MI: Eerdmans.

Goldingay, J. 2003. *Old Testament Theology*. Downers Grove, IL: InterVarsity Press.

Green, C. E. 2010. "The Crucified God and the Groaning Spirit: Toward a Pentecostal *Theologia Crucis* in Conversation with Jürgen Moltman." *Journal of Pentecostal Theology* 19, no. 1: 28–30.

Hamilton, V. P. 2005. *Handbook on the Pentateuch*. 2nd ed. Grand Rapids, MI: Baker Academic.

Hill, A. E. 1986. "Prosperity." In G. W. Bromiley, ed., *The International Standard Bible Encyclopedia*, 3:1011–12. Grand Rapids, MI: Eerdmans.

Hymns for Malawi. 1975. Blantyre: CLAIM

Peels, H. G. L. 2003. *Shadow Sides: The Revelation of God in the Old Testament*. Carlisle: Paternoster.

Preuss, H. D. 1995. *Old Testament Theology*. Vol. 2. Edinburgh: T&T Clark.

Rendtorf, R. 2005. *The Canonical Hebrew Bible: A Theology of the Old Testament*. Leiden: Deo.

Rouse, T. 1999. *Faith and the Pharisees*. Tulsa: Insight Publishing Group.

Schmidt, W. H. 1999. *Old Testament: Introduction*. 2nd ed. Louisville, KY: Westminster John Knox Press.

Walton, J., and A. E. Hill. 2004. *Old Testament Today: A Journey from Original Meaning to Contemporary Significance*. Grand Rapids, MI: Zondervan.

3

Is the Prosperity Gospel Biblical?
A Critique in Light of Literary Context and Union with Christ

DUSTIN W. ELLINGTON

THE GOSPEL OF HEALTH and wealth proclaims that God promises physical healing and financial prosperity in this lifetime to those who trust and follow God's ways. This message is powerfully alluring for Zambia and surrounding countries, where people face poverty and sickness beyond what much of the world has ever seen. From what one observes at the grassroots level, the gospel of health and wealth may be becoming the most popular and core message of the Christian faith, so that the prosperity gospel becomes *the gospel* of this part of Africa.

This situation may seem alarming or hard to believe for Christians in Europe and North America, but it must be remembered that a large chasm lies between the daily experience of most Africans and most Westerners. Zambians are hungry for development, progress, and success; in comparison, most Americans and Europeans have already experienced these things. Europeans and North Americans tend to take it for granted that their physical needs will normally be met, so they hardly connect the meeting of these basic needs with their life of faith. In contrast, Africans tend not

Part 2: BIBLICAL ANALYSIS

to take it for granted that they will have access to such basic needs as food, medical care, and education, and they connect the obtaining of their needs with their newfound Christian faith. Sufficient access to food, health, and education has tended to elude Africans, but they are beginning to believe that it is possible to flourish, and that God cares to give them what they need to be able to do so. Africans have long observed the relative wealth of Westerners living in their countries, and many Africans have also grown wealthy in recent years as their nations' economies have grown. These realities stir curiosity about just how much success God might wish to provide. In such an environment, striking the right balance between the belief that God cares for their well-being, and the belief that believers' prosperity is the point and promise of the Christian life, is a considerable challenge. To serve the ongoing dialogue toward teaching truth in the African church, what follows will address two major concerns regarding the prosperity gospel.

One concern is that the message of prosperity does not reflect what Scripture really teaches, and that most believers' level of skill in reading the Bible for themselves does not equip them to recognize this problem. Unfortunately, the debate regarding whether or not the message of prosperity is biblical tends to remain at the level of each side lining up proof texts for its own point of view and casting them at the other side. This article seeks to take the debate to a higher level by inviting believers to look not just at proof texts but also at the main aims, themes, and lines of thought of biblical books and of the canon of Scripture as a whole. The wider literary context of biblical verses clarifies their meaning and places responsible limitations on their use. This article will propose that the prosperity gospel must come to terms with, and be greatly adjusted by, Scripture's key themes, aims, and lines of thought, both within individual biblical books and, more broadly, in the biblical canon as a whole. Training African believers to read the Bible in its own literary context, so as to recognize the main themes and lines of thought, will help them to see weaknesses in the prosperity gospel and come to a balanced view of what Scripture teaches about suffering and flourishing.

The other concern is that, in its reliance on proof texts for its point of view, the prosperity gospel neglects a theme which is absolutely central for the Christian life: believers' union with Christ and the impact of Jesus's death on the Christian life which results from this union. Christ's death brings a union between Christ and believers that leads believers to follow Christ's own pattern of life, and that pattern tends to involve suffering and self-renunciation. In its teaching on the Christian life, the prosperity gospel fails to take the cross of Christ into account. This article points to the neglect of the cross and union with Christ as a critical example of how the prosperity gospel makes frequent use of Scriptural proof texts but tends to miss the spirit of the Bible as a whole.[1]

Finally, the article will suggest that the weaknesses of the prosperity gospel argue for investing in rigorous theological training on the African continent that highlights teaching believers to interpret Scripture in its literary and canonical context. This will lead to responsible interpretation of the Bible and a realization of the significance of Christ's death for the lives of believers. The upshot will be Scripture-shaped teaching and living among Africa's Christians.

Responsible Interpretation of the Bible

Prosperity Preachers' Proof Texts

Is the gospel of prosperity biblical? That is, does it communicate what Scripture itself teaches, and does it express what is true of the Bible as a whole?

Certainly those who preach prosperity present it as a message from Scripture. They point to a wide array of key verses that seem to guarantee financial breakthroughs. For instance, prosperity preachers repeatedly quote 2 Corinthians 8–9, including: "For you know the grace of our Lord Jesus Christ, that though he was rich, yet for your sakes he became poor, so that you through his poverty might become rich" (2 Cor 8:9). They also repeat, "And God is able to make all grace abound to you, so that in all things at all times, having all that you need, you will abound in every good work" (2 Cor 9:8).[2]

However, these verses which prosperity preachers quote tend to be removed from their original context of 2 Corinthians. This is one of

---

1. While it is beyond the purview of this article, the author's suspicion is that by using biblical proof texts and yet neglecting the heart of what Scripture is about, the prosperity gospel is able to take themes and values from both secularism and African traditional religions and, perhaps unwittingly, dress them up in Christian and biblical language. Thus the prosperity gospel may sound Christian even while it is, in essence, something different.

2. One prosperity preacher commended to me by Zambians is Singapore's Joseph Prince. His ministry's webpage on prosperity and provision repeatedly quotes 2 Corinthians. See JosephPrince.org.

Part 2: BIBLICAL ANALYSIS

the biblical books most quoted by prosperity preachers, but as a whole it teaches something very different than the prosperity gospel. It is the same letter where the Apostle says twice that he has often gone hungry (2 Cor 6:5; 11:27) and where he teaches that the sufferings of Christ are abundant in the lives of believers (2 Cor 1:5). It is also in 2 Corinthians that Paul tells of the thorn in his flesh that would not leave him, despite his repeated pleas to God (2 Cor 12:7–10). In fact, one of the main themes of 2 Corinthians is that the Christian life is *not* about escaping or moving beyond weakness and suffering (Ellington 2012: 340). For this reason, it is quite strange to use verses from 2 Corinthians to guarantee material success to believers.

If 2 Corinthians as a whole does not promise prosperity to believers, then how is it that prosperity preachers keep turning to 2 Corinthians for promises of financial breakthrough? The answer lies in their interpretive method: They tend to rely upon scattered verses in the New Testament that are removed from their original context, and they tend to overlook the main aims, major lines of thought, and key themes of biblical books from where the verses originate. Prosperity preachers' removal of verses from where they originate leads them to misinterpret the verses they quote. In the case of 2 Corinthians, the result is a contradiction of the overall message of the book. Preachers need to be careful about relying upon a few scattered Bible verses pulled out of their historical and literary context. They need to be wary of utilizing these as proof texts that run against the main themes of the books of the Bible where they were originally found. Yet this is precisely the error that many who preach the message of prosperity fall into.

Understanding communication, and interpreting it wisely, always requires context. Imagine trying to view an impressionist painting by looking at only a few of the artist's dots, while ignoring the whole. Or imagine the proverbial blind person trying to describe an elephant by touching only one part of its body. In both cases, the resulting picture is quite different than reality. The same might be said of prosperity preachers' approach to quoting the Bible.

Literary Context

The prevalence and progress of the prosperity gospel is partly due to Christians' failure to understand verses of the Bible in their original literary context. What does it mean to read Scripture in light of the literary context, and why is the literary context so important?

By giving attention to the "literary context," I mean that we interpret words in light of the verses of the Bible in which they are found. And we interpret verses in light of the immediate sections of Scripture in which they're found. And we interpret small sections of verses in light of chapters and larger sections of a book of the Bible. And we interpret chapters and larger sections of a book of the Bible in light of the book as a whole. Words, sentences, passages, and chapters "take their meaning from the biblical book of which they are a part" (Brown 2007:213).[3] In short, making use of the literary context means that we interpret words and verses according to what we find in the immediate and surrounding passages, and we interpret these smaller parts in light of what we see in a book of Scripture as a whole.

The literary context is important because it keeps us on track by setting interpretive limits and clarifying the possible range of meaning for a verse of the Bible. It is true that we all bring ideologies and concerns that affect our interpretation of a text. This is unavoidable to a degree, but too often we force a piece of Scripture to fit our preconceived notions. This occurs with few limits, resulting in any number of possible meanings, if we do not read in context. Yet when we read a verse in its literary context, we have to face what is really in the text, which makes it much more difficult to compel Scripture to say whatever we want it to say. When we read a verse in its literary context, we must deal with the verse in light of what the rest of its own context is saying. While it is very hard to see the meaning of a text if we do not understand what the author says before and after that given piece of text, the literary context gives us much to work with, because we have the author's own guidance to clarify the meaning. A good literary approach allows Scripture to have its own voice rather than being dictated strictly by the concerns of the reader.

Let us look at a real-life example. On more than one occasion I have heard Zambian preachers discuss whether or not Jesus's promise of abundant life in the Gospel of John should encourage them to dream of owning their own airplanes. The debate concerns this verse: "The thief comes only to steal and kill and destroy. I came that they may have life, and have it abundantly" (John 10:10 NRSV). In the contemporary context of Africa's preachers, where the prosperity gospel thrives, and where a preacher's personal wealth is a sign of God's blessing, true abundance might look like owning one's own airplane. However, from the perspective of using the

---

3. I recommend Brown's *Scripture as Communication* for an initial study of hermeneutics, along with Thiselton, *Hermeneutics*.

Part 2: BIBLICAL ANALYSIS

literary context of Scripture, questions of the contemporary context are not the first or only ones that matter. The literary approach asks the question: What does abundant life mean in the Gospel of John? "Life" is one of the main themes of that gospel, so by tracing how it uses and speaks of the word "life," we can arrive at a fairly clear idea of what these words mean in their original literary context. This should clarify and put limits on the contemporary discussion of whether pastors should seek to own their own airplanes. By looking at how John's gospel uses the word "life," we can see that it tends to mean "eternal life," and yet eternal life begins now through our faith and knowledge of God. One only needs a Bible concordance to see where and how Jesus speaks of life in John's gospel; then a reader can discern the extent to which Jesus has material goods in mind when Jesus speaks of life abundant.

Some readers may be cautious about our ability to be sure of what Scripture really teaches. Can a person be certain that the Bible actually teaches for or against the prosperity gospel? Some may claim: Are not our readings contextual and largely determined by our point of view and attitudes which we have before we pick up the Bible and read? Some might ask this question because they wish to avoid the authority of Scripture in their personal lifestyle, but many others genuinely wonder about these questions.

Certainly, all readings of Scripture bear the influence of our contemporary context and the lens of experience and ideology through which we read. There is no such thing as an entirely objective reading. However, while the limitations of a reader and his or her context put limits on his or her interpretation, interpretation is not simply or only shaped by the reader's context. The writers of Scripture did not leave us in the dark in regard to their main aims and themes, and we can trace them by learning to read well. We can gain confidence about discovering what Scripture says by learning to use its literary context. As we use the literary context, we can hold the content of what we find in the Bible in dialogue with our situation on the ground in Africa. This helps us to hear how the content of Scripture addresses our contemporary context.

Canonical Context

Some readers might grant the argument so far but argue that the prosperity gospel is a key theme spread throughout much of the Old Testament, and especially the book of Deuteronomy. Indeed, in support of the message of prosperity, Deuteronomy does teach that God blesses the obedient with material prosperity. This is at the heart of Deuteronomy's theology. When Deuteronomy 28:2 says, "All these blessings shall come upon you and overtake you, if you obey the LORD your God," it is more than a proof text, and the wider literary context of the book demonstrates that material blessings are included. The verse communicates what Deuteronomy is actually about, and this theology can be found scattered in the Old Testament's literature.[4]

While this article grants that prosperity as a reward for obedience is a genuine principal theme of Deuteronomy, and that we find this idea in a wide variety of Old Testament books, the trouble is that prosperity preachers take this theme and make it a *guarantee* for believers today to receive material blessing, without observing the way the rest of the biblical canon puts limits on this teaching and prevents it from being a guarantee in every case. Failure to observe the way the rest of the canon qualifies and nuances its teaching is a hallmark of the prosperity gospel. The meaning of a verse of Scripture should be understood in light of the book of the Bible in which it is found; in addition, we need to observe the canonical context when we preach something as a general truth. For a teaching to be considered crucial enough to repeat day after day and week after week, as the prosperity gospel is proclaimed in Africa, it must stand the test of what we discover in the rest of the canon, which is crucial for determining the church's main teachings.

Filtering the prosperity gospel through the New Testament would mean qualifying the message substantially, but the canon of the Old Testament also requires that we nuance this message. The Psalms of lament, for example, sometimes present the Psalmist as one who is righteous and yet suffers. Psalm 44:15, 17–19, and 23–24 state:

> My disgrace is before me all day long, and my face is covered with shame . . . All this happened to us, though we had not forgotten you or been false to your covenant. Our hearts had not turned back; our feet had not strayed from your path. But you crushed us and made us a haunt for jackals and covered us over with deep darkness . . . Awake, O Lord! Why do you sleep? Rouse yourself! Do not reject us forever. Why do you hide your face and forget our misery and oppression?

---

4. The website of Joseph Prince Ministries, under the heading "Prosperity and Provision Confession," quotes Deuteronomy 28 and 2 Corinthians 8–9 more than other texts of Scripture (Joseph Prince Ministries 2013). See http://www.josephprince.org/Resources_Confess_The_Word_Provision.html?active=resources.

Part 2: BIBLICAL ANALYSIS

Along similar lines, Psalm 73:13–14 gives voice to the reality that sometimes the faithful suffer: surely in vain have I kept my heart pure; in vain have I washed my hands in innocence. All day long I have been plagued; I have been punished every morning. Yet the same Psalm affirms: "Whom have I in heaven but you? And earth has nothing I desire besides you. My flesh and my heart may fail, but God is the strength of my heart and my portion forever" (Ps 73:25–26).

It is not only the Psalms which call the guarantee of prosperity into question. Job is a righteous sufferer. Isaiah 53, a chapter which came to hold significance for the early Christians' understanding of Jesus, speaks of the righteous servant who suffers. The prophet Jeremiah was faithful and yet suffered. While material blessings often come to the righteous in the Old Testament, it is not uncommon that the righteous suffer.

In light of these realities, relying on the Old Testament canon as a whole, a preacher cannot guarantee physical blessings to believers in return for their obedience. Physical blessings as a reward for obedience is one of the ways God works; the Old Testament also presents other very different ways God deals with the faithful. As Ellen Davis states, "The Bible is rigorously realistic in its representations of human character, the conditions and contingencies of life in this world. Therefore the aim of Old Testament preaching is to invite Christians to grow toward spiritual maturity in circumstances that are always less than ideal" (2012:1).

Learning the Skill of Analysis

One reason for the prosperity gospel's success in Africa is that Christians receive a steady diet of this gospel from the television and the radio, and few people have the tools and preparation to evaluate the message as to whether or not it is biblical. When students arrive at our institution, they are comfortable with listening to lectures and reading books to receive and pass on information, but most have not been exposed to education that teaches them to analyze what they read. When new students prepare a sermon, they tend to be at a loss when asked to do personal analysis of a biblical text. Instead of analyzing their passage of the Bible, the tendency is to copy what a Bible commentary says about their passage and then begin to think for themselves about the practical application. When they neglect the personal analysis of Scripture for themselves, they demonstrate a lack of confidence and skill in interpretation of Scripture. Relatively few people have gained the ability to trace the line of thought within biblical books and see the variety of nuances contained in passages of Scripture. But if theological colleges teach students the skill of analyzing a text (any text), and they learn to apply that skill to the Bible, then they will be able to see for themselves the extent to which the gospel of prosperity rings true with the themes and aims of the Bible.

To assure that teaching is biblical, preachers and teachers must learn to identify the main aims, themes, and lines of thought in the writings of Scripture for themselves. We can learn to do this in individual passages, in individual books of the Bible, and in the canon as a whole. The result is that as teachers and preachers we know that what we teach matches what the Bible is really about, because we see our teaching emphasized as main themes in whole streams of thought, represented in large sections of Scripture. And where a teaching is nuanced by other lines of thought, we need to admit that and not give guarantees that God automatically works in one way instead of another.

When preachers learn to interpret individual verses in light of the larger pieces of Scripture in which they are found, the result is that they will be able to tell the difference between a proof text taken out of context and a statement or verse that represents what Scripture as a whole teaches. This is of great value when evaluating the prosperity gospel or any other teaching.

While God may bless believers with prosperity, this is not affirmed throughout Scripture. Therefore it cannot be taught as something that is automatic and mechanical as so many prosperity preachers guarantee. To be a central message of the church and a true interpretation of the Christian life, a teaching must square with main lines of thought in the biblical canon, and it should not violate the main lines of thought of the biblical writings from which verses are quoted. The prosperity gospel must be held in dialogue with, and critiqued by, the themes of Scripture which anyone may observe to be genuinely central. The next section aims to do just that by focusing on one such theme, the union between Christ and believers.

Part 2: BIBLICAL ANALYSIS

Union with Christ and the Life of Believers

The Centre of Paul's Thought about the Christian Life

Although a few wealthy believers appear in the New Testament,[5] the books of the New Testament appear to have no vision for believers pursuing a surplus of material wealth to enjoy as God's blessing in this lifetime. It is important to ask why this is so. The proposed answer is that the death of Jesus Christ exerts a profound influence upon the way the New Testament portrays the Christian life. The New Testament depicts the life of believers as one of union with Jesus Christ, a union made possible through Jesus's death and resurrection. This union with Christ involves a whole new way of life for believers, and it is not a life marked by material prosperity; in fact, it is lived on behalf of others and tends to involve suffering in order to reveal Christ to the world.

This article argued above that for a teaching of the Christian life to be central and one that Christians return to frequently and repeatedly, it must express what we find among the main themes and lines of thought in the biblical canon. One of the key themes of the New Testament, especially in regard to its teaching on the Christian life, is believers' union with Christ. One can study the various expressions of this theme in any major section of the New Testament, but this article will focus on union with Christ in Paul's thought.[6]

Two of the most influential twentieth-century interpreters of the Apostle Paul were Albert Schweitzer and E. P. Sanders. The writings of both assert that union with Christ is the centre of Paul's theology.[7] They use different terms to refer to it, with Schweitzer preferring the term "Christ

---

5. When Paul describes the Corinthian congregation, he says "not many" of their members were powerful or of noble birth, suggesting that some were. Those hosting house churches, like Philemon (Philemon 1–2), might also have been affluent. James 5:1 seems to address wealthy believers.

6. The language of the Synoptic Gospels is different than that of the rest of the New Testament in this regard, but their terminology of discipleship and following Jesus also expresses a form of union with Christ. The heavy preoccupation upon Jesus's death in the synoptic narratives (frequently dubbed "passion narratives with extended introductions") also signals the deep importance of the death of Jesus for the Christian life. Cf. also Luke 14:27, "Whoever does not carry the cross and follow me cannot be my disciple" (NRSV).

7. Schweitzer 1931:3, 22. See the discussions in Sanders 1977:434–41, and 1983:4–10.

mysticism"[8] and Sanders "participation in Christ,"[9] but both scholars refer to the union with Christ made possible for believers through Jesus's death on the cross and resurrection. Schweitzer and Sanders argue that union with Christ is the centre of Paul's thought on the basis of its being more frequently mentioned than other topics, including justification by faith, and also because the apostle explains Christian behavior on the grounds of believers being in Christ and Christ being in believers.[10] While scholars disagree as to whether union with Christ is the centre of Paul's theology, it is difficult to argue against the proposition that union between Christ and believers is the heart and generating centre of Paul's thought *about the Christian life*.

Paul's Description of Union with Christ

Because union with Christ is one of the most prominent themes of the New Testament and one that raises difficulties for the prosperity gospel's teaching on the Christian life, it is worthwhile to examine the concept in some detail. While Paul's language describing union with Christ may be readily seen in all the letters which bear his name, this article will focus especially on 1–2 Corinthians.

We can gain a more complete understanding of union with Christ by turning to Paul's own words to the Corinthians. To describe the concept of believers' union with Christ, Paul most commonly speaks of us being "in

---

8. Concerning Schweitzer's use of this term, Anthony Thiselton states: "It would be a mistake to over-react to the use of the word 'mysticism.' As Sanders points out: 'His term "mysticism" has been rejected by scholars . . . on the basis of definitions which Schweitzer himself would not have accepted'" (1979:136). Thiselton quotes Sanders 1977:459. Schweitzer's interpretation of Paul does raise other concerns. He places too great an emphasis on sharing in a corporeity with the *resurrection* at the present time (1931:111, 116). Paul places greater emphasis, in the present tense, on sharing in Christ's death: He and his partners model for the Corinthians a life of always carrying in the body the death of Jesus (2 Cor 4:10). Schweitzer also overstates the power and importance of predestination in Paul's thought (9, 103). He does the same with the importance of baptism in contrast to faith as establishing union with Christ (117, 128). Finally, Schweitzer was also mistaken when he asserted that a believer loses "his creatively individual existence and his natural personality" (125). For Sanders's comments on weaknesses in Schweitzer's interpretation, see 1977:434, 440.

9. See 1977:435–41. Sanders labels Paul's theology "participationist eschatology" (1977:549).

10. See Sanders 1977: 439. Schweitzer demonstrated that believers' being in Christ was the source of their ethical life (1931: 220, 295).

Part 2: BIBLICAL ANALYSIS

Christ,"[11] and having Christ "in us." As a consequence of Christ's death and resurrection, those who believe (1 Cor 15:1–2; cf. Gal 3:2; 3:26–27) and are baptised (1 Cor 12:13; cf. Rom 6:3–4) are in a relationship that involves, in some genuine sense, an overlapping space with Christ and the Spirit. Thus, believers are now "in Christ." Paul addresses the Corinthian believers as though they reside in two parallel locations: "in Corinth," yet set apart in Christ Jesus (1 Cor 1:2).

Paul speaks of an overlapping location in yet other ways. He says that believers' bodies are members of Christ (1 Cor 6:15); they are joined with Christ and become one spirit with him (1 Cor 6:17). Together, believers compose "the body of Christ"[12] (1 Cor 12:27). Through their connection with Christ, "the many are one body" (1 Cor 10:17). Moreover, through the physical location of the bread and cup in the Lord's Supper, a *koinōnia* (a fellowship or participation) in Christ's death, occurs. Paul also says that he and his partners contain or "carry around the death of Jesus in the body, in order that the life of Jesus may be manifest in our body" (2 Cor 4:10). Furthermore, Paul explains that instead of being ashamed of his weaknesses, he boasts about them, "in order that the power of Christ may dwell in me" (2 Cor 12:9). And when he claims he has worked harder than the other apostles, he says it was, "not I, but the grace of God with me" (15:10). Grace, as the power of the Lord, works alongside Paul, closely enough to be the true subject of his action. Paul's locative language reflects the depth of union between Christ and believers, and the widely varying images and terminology denote the pervasiveness and importance of this union.

---

11. Since Paul so pervasively describes believers as overlapping in their location with Christ, it makes the most sense to take Paul's phrase *en Christō* as principally locative—genuinely describing believers' location. So also Deissman 1926:297–98. See also John Schütz 1975:207–8; and Anthony C. Thiselton 2000:76. The dative case may at times include an instrumental sense as well. See Wolfgang Schrage 1995:1, 103, 114. So also Thiselton 2000:76.

12. Schweitzer aids us in seeing that "in Christ" is oriented to the social plane as well as to participation in Jesus Christ (1931:123). We should also remember Ernst Käsemann's point that being "in Christ" signifies Christ's dominion, which is manifested through the bodies of his followers, even if Käsemann mistakenly emphasizes dominion to the exclusion of other participatory notions (1964:68).

Union with Christ, Suffering, and the Moral Life

For Paul, because Christ suffered in his body, those who live in union with Christ also experience hardship. Union with Christ impacts the embodied nature of our lives, so that we go through suffering in this life. "The sufferings of Christ abound to us" (2 Cor 1:5), and: "Now if we are children, then we are heirs—heirs—heirs of God and co-heirs with Christ, if indeed we share in his sufferings in order that we may also share in his glory" (Rom 8:17). Moreover, "He was crucified because of weakness . . . We also are weak in him" (2 Cor 13:4). And, "We are always being handed over to death because of Jesus" (2 Cor 4:11; cf. 4:7; 13:4; Phil 1:29). We participate in Christ's power of resurrection in this life ("inwardly we are being renewed every day"), but as far as our physical life on this earth is concerned, our connection with the crucifixion seems stronger and more determinative ("outwardly we are wasting away," 2 Cor 4:16; and, "in this dwelling we groan, longing to be clothed with our dwelling from heaven," 2 Cor 5:2).

Union with Christ is also that which shapes the moral life of believers and enables us to live for Christ and for others. Participation in Christ serves as the key basis and enabling force of the believing community's moral life. For Paul, those who are in Christ have a distinct manner of life, shaped by Christ's death and resurrection.[13] Paul says that Christ "died for all, that those who live would live no longer for themselves but for him who died for them and rose again" (2 Cor 5:15). Moreover, immediately before Paul begins to deal practically with the Corinthian congregation's fault of disunity and call them to be of the same mind, he tells them they have been called into the "fellowship (*koinōnia*) of God's Son" (1 Cor 1:9). Similarly, Paul tells the Corinthians to "flee immorality" (1 Cor 6:18) and "glorify God in your body" (6:20), after describing the ways that their bodies are members of Christ and one spirit with him. According to Schweitzer, Paul derives his ethic solely from the character of the new state of existence which results from the dying and rising again with Christ and the bestowal of the Spirit" (1931:297). Schweitzer says of the phrase "in Christ": "It is no mere formula for Paul. For him every manifestation of the life of the baptized man is conditioned by his being in Christ" (1931:125).

---

13. Sanders states: "One participates in salvation by becoming one person with Christ . . . his behaviour should be determined by his new situation" (1977: 549). See also Tannehill 1967:77–83.

Part 2: BIBLICAL ANALYSIS

Union with Christ and the Gospel Leads to a Life of Mission

Paul teaches and models for the Corinthians a union not only with Christ but also with the gospel he proclaims. The gospel is more than a message to preach; it is also an advancing force,[14] a power that takes on its own life in the community of faith, bringing salvation and reconciliation as it moves. Through his example, Paul continually challenges the Corinthians to become one with the gospel's pattern and power, so that instead of standing in the gospel's way (1 Cor 9:12), they let it shape them to act on behalf of the salvation of others. Paul's life is one of personal adjustments and self-sacrificial actions for others (9:19–23). Instead of seeking his own advantage, he acts on behalf of others, so that they may be saved (10:33). Paul sums up his personal adjustments and self-sacrifice by saying he aims to be a *sungkoinōnos*, a partner and participant, in the gospel's pattern and its power to save (9:23). His exhortation to imitate himself in 11:1 calls the congregation to share in this special relationship with the gospel (Ellington 2011), so that they embrace the vocation that arises from union with the gospel. In practical terms, this leads believers to relinquish personal privileges for the sake of the gospel's advance. What a contrast exists between Paul's words and those of prosperity preachers who defend their wealth as sign of God's blessing.

Paul's conception of union with Christ serves as the foundation for the church's mission of visibly representing the gospel to the world.[15] Paul believes that Christian proclamation is not only through preaching (1 Cor 1:17–18) or the Lord's Supper (1 Cor 11:26), but through the ongoing, holistic life of believers. Paul models the gospel with his life in order to teach the church to do the same. Union with Christ leads to the embodied expression of the gospel, and enables believers, not just apostles, to manifest the gospel through their daily life.[16] Participation in Christ becomes visible in the embodied life of individual believers and a congregation as a whole.

---

14. So also Schütz 1975:53.

15. See Sunquist's *Understanding Christian Mission*.

16. It is of critical importance that Paul does not think this phenomenon of embodying the gospel is unique to him as an apostle. He understands his own calling to embody the gospel in light of the calling of the church as a whole. This moderates Paul's apostolic uniqueness, leaving a thin, penetrable boundary between apostles and the rest of the church. I argue this point in an unpublished paper, "Revisiting Paul's 'We' in 2 Corinthians 4: A Shared Vocation through Participation in Christ," presented to the New Testament Society of South Africa in August of 2011. Cf. Ellington 2012:342.

Paul carries the message of Christ as a treasure in the earthen vessel of his body (2 Cor 4:7). As believers go through difficulty, their embodied experience reveals the life of Jesus; they "are always carrying the dying of Jesus in the body, in order that the life of Jesus may also be manifest in the body." The message of reconciliation has been "placed in us" (*themenos en hēmin*) (2 Cor 5:19)—that is, in our bodies, our embodied life. Believers are also the fragrance of Christ among those being saved and among the perishing (2 Cor 2:15). We are, moreover, "a letter from Christ" (2 Cor 3:3). Because of our union with Christ and the gospel, the Christian life is a picture of the good news of Christ's death for others. The Christian life must not contradict this pattern and message.

Union with Christ and the Prosperity Gospel

Since, like union with Christ, the prosperity gospel is a teaching on the Christian life, it is important to hold the two themes in dialogue with one another. The prosperity gospel teaches individuals that material success is their destiny on earth. Inasmuch as it mentions the cross at all, the prosperity gospel capitalizes on the idea that because Jesus Christ suffered, believers do not need to suffer.

The trouble is that this line of thought does not square with the New Testament's teaching on the Christian life as lived in union with Christ. The Bible does teach that Christ's death paid for our sins, so that we do not bear the burden of suffering death as a punishment. But Christ's death is also the means for us to be brought into a real union with Christ, so that his death and life become our own lived experience. Paul's letters describe a Christian vocation of living by the cross, a calling that is rooted in and shaped by believers' union with the crucified and risen Jesus Christ. (A longer article could demonstrate the same belief in other sections of the New Testament.)[17] Believers' lives are always marked by the reality of Jesus Christ's death for others, but the gospel of prosperity tends either to overlook this reality or to misconstrue it. The passages cited above demonstrate that the death of Jesus has profound influence on the way the Christian life is lived out. We believers carry Christ's suffering in our own bodily experience of this life, so that the life of Jesus will be revealed to the world (2 Cor 4:10–11).

17. Richard B. Hays's inclusion of the cross as one of three key metaphors of Christian ethics throughout the New Testament is indicative of this reality (Hays 1996).

Part 2: BIBLICAL ANALYSIS

Our examination of union with Christ has unveiled deep contrasts between it and the gospel of prosperity. The death of Jesus holds such powerful sway over believers' lives in the New Testament that the pursuit of wealth as an end in itself does not surface as a viable option for believers. This is why, if one turns to the New Testament in search of the prosperity gospel, it is difficult to find.

Conclusions for Theological Education in Africa

The Bible does not guarantee prosperity for believers in this lifetime. This does not mean that God discourages human enjoyment of life on earth or wishes people to live in poverty. God created the world and called it good (Gen 1:31). Later, God saw the misery of his people enslaved in Egypt, felt compassion, and promised to deliver them from those circumstances (Ex 3:7–8). God cares about people's earthly well-being. The stance of this article is also not that the message of prosperity contains no biblical support. Sometimes God gives wealth to believers during this lifetime. Rather, the critique is that the prosperity gospel misreads what Scripture is truly about and that it misrepresents the Bible when it guarantees prosperity in this lifetime. Much of Scripture, especially the New Testament's emphasis on union with Christ, teaches something quite different about believers' experience of life in this world.

This misrepresentation could be avoided by a more responsible and thoughtful approach to the interpretation of the Bible. We have observed the importance of teaching exegetical skills, which help students see for themselves what is really present in Bible verses, biblical books, and the canon of Scripture as a whole. Those who train pastors and teachers of the church are challenged to require that students learn to carry out the study of Bible verses and biblical passages in their literary and canonical context. If future pastors learn to do this, Scripture will be allowed to have a voice for itself, and interpretation will not be left solely to the dictates of personal and societal pressures. This will help students, preachers, and their congregations to progress toward thinking biblically for their own contexts. They will be able hold biblical theology in honest dialogue with African realities, instead of being "tossed back and forth . . . and blown here and there by every wind of teaching" (Eph 4:14). The goal is for believers to be able to see what is in Scripture and then think through and live out a scripturally shaped way of life in the African context.

Finally, we have seen how one of the main themes of the New Testament, union with Christ, raises serious questions for the prosperity gospel. The prosperity gospel's tendency to use the Bible as a source of proof texts, as opposed to interpreting verses in light of their literary and canonical context, leads people to overlook crucial aspects of the Christian life. The New Testament teaches that our union with Christ leads us to embody his death for others through our way of life. This contradicts seeing the Christian life as a means for obtaining personal wealth. Let us heed Jesus's words: "If anyone would come after me, he must deny himself and take up his cross and follow me" (Matt 16:24; Mark 8:34; Luke 9:23).

Bibliography

Brown, Jeannine K. 2007. *Scripture as Communication: Introducing Biblical Hermeneutics.* Grand Rapids, MI: Baker Academic.

Davis, Ellen F. 2012. "Witnessing to God in the Midst of Life: Old Testament Preaching." *Expository Times* 124 (Oct.): 1–8.

Deissmann, Adolf. 1926. *Paul: A Study in Social and Religious History.* Translated by W. E. Wilson. New York: Doran.

Ellington, Dustin W. 2011. "Imitating Paul's Relationship to the Gospel: 1 Cor 8:1–11:1." *Journal for the Study of the New Testament* 33, no. 3:303–15.

———. 2012. "Not Applicable to Believers? The Aims and Basis of Paul's 'I' in 2 Corinthians 10–13." *Journal of Biblical Literature* 131, no. 2:327–42.

Hays, Richard B. 1996. *The Moral Vision of the New Testament: Community, Cross, New Creation.* San Francisco: Harper.

Joseph Prince Ministries. 2013. "Provision Confessions." Joseph Prince Ministries [online]. Available at: http://www.josephprince.org/Resources_Confess_The_Word_Provision.html?active=resources.

Käsemann, Ernst. 1964. "Ministry and Community in the New Testament." In E. Käsemann, *Essays on New Testament Themes,* 63–94. Translated by W. J. Montague. London: SCM, 1964.

Sanders, E. P. 1977. *Paul and Palestinian Judaism: A Comparison of Patterns of Religion.* Minneapolis: Fortress.

———. 1983. *Paul, the Law, and the Jewish People.* Minneapolis: Fortress.

Schrage, Wolfgang. 1995. *Der erste Brief an die Korinther.* Düsseldorf: Benziger Verlag.

Schütz, John Howard. 2007 [1975]. *Paul and the Anatomy of Apostolic Authority.* Louisville: Westminster John Knox.

Schweitzer, Albert, 1998 [1931]. *The Mysticism of Paul the Apostle.* Translated by W. Montgomery. Baltimore: Johns Hopkins.

Sunquist, Scott. 2013. *Understanding Christian Mission: Participation in Suffering and Glory.* Grand Rapids, MI: Baker Academic.

Tannehill, Robert. 1967. *Dying and Rising with Christ: A Study in Pauline Theology.* Berlin: Töpelmann.

Part 2: BIBLICAL ANALYSIS

Thiselton, Anthony C. 1979. "Schweitzer's Interpretation of Paul." *Expository Times* 90 (Feb.): 132–37.
———. 2000. *The First Epistle to the Corinthians*. Grand Rapids, MI: Eerdmans.
———. 2009. *Hermeneutics: An Introduction*. Grand Rapids, MI: Eerdmans.

PART 3

Theological Reflection

4

Jesus the Healer

DEVISON TELEN BANDA

To ACKNOWLEDGE JESUS AS a healer, some understanding is important. A healer can be perceived to be a person or a corporate entity that brings or facilitates health and wellbeing. A healer cures the sick, the afflicted or those experiencing brokenness, although health means much more than the mere absence of disease. Every healer engages people in need, and where individual or corporate brokenness is involved the healer tries to achieve restoration. It is important to note that wellbeing means much more than the mere absence of illness. By engaging the vulnerable the healer is a peacemaker and relationship builder, because the community of the healed joins in celebrating the much-needed healing event. Health or wellbeing is thus an essential part of human existence. In the African context, where life expectancy has dropped to the forties, when people's health is threatened, they become desperate and their desperation renders them vulnerable to many things. In search of healing, people are ready to try anything. In order to bring about healing, the healer assumes some kind of mediating power, usually drawn from some supreme power. The healer or medicine man or woman is not tied to one methodology through which to discharge his or her functions.

Part 3: THEOLOGICAL REFLECTION

Perspectives on Healing

Healing is an essential aspect of health or general wellbeing. To appreciate the place of healing, it is important to understand the basic notion of health. What is health? Although there may be various competing definitions, generally health is a holistic state of wellbeing. It covers the physical, mental, moral and spiritual aspects of humanity. As whole beings, humans are wired in such a way that when a single aspect of the person lacks health, the whole being is affected. Health rests at the core of human existence because it affects culture, education, socio-economic development, morality, spirituality, and any other essential aspect of humanness that one may consider.

Perhaps this is the reason why, in the developed world, health insurance is a major part of living. Everyone is required to have functioning insurance so that whenever health is threatened, interventions can be put in place in good time. In the American 2012 presidential election, health policies were a major campaign issue and there is a general belief that such policies, which candidates openly debated, had a huge bearing on the voting, especially in the swing states and among minority groups.

In many African cultures there is a strong belief that illness, or lack of health, is a messenger of death. It is not an exaggeration to say that the sub-Saharan region is not only one of the poorest regions of the world but is also under the siege of many kinds of diseases. Even though many African, or sub-Saharan cultures in particular, stress the belief that "The trees of the future are in the seed of today," or, directly relating to humans: "Children are the future of every nation," our region is among regions of the world where infant mortality is high. This can be confirmed by the 2012 World Health Organization report which in part states:

> Globally, significant progress has been made in reducing mortality rates among children under five years old. Between 1990 and 2010, the under-five mortality rate declined by 35%—from an estimated 88 deaths per 1000 live births to 57. The global rate of decline has also accelerated in recent years—from 2.1% per annum during 1990–2010 to 2.6% during 2005–2010 . . . The annual rate of decline in the WHO African Region—where almost half of all child deaths occur—increased from 1.8% during 1990–2010 to 2.8% during 2005–2010. Despite this improvement, most countries in the Region are unlikely to achieve the MDG target of a two-thirds reduction in 1990 mortality levels by the year 2015 (2012:12).

One aspect of interest from the above extract is that the report mentions the "WHO African Region." It may not be reading too much into the statement to believe that the report is about data captured by the World Health Organization (WHO). African realities are unfortunately of such a nature that rural populations away from health facilities are hard to be captured in any survey even if they form a dominant child population. One would hope that even if the report of experts expresses the doubt in meeting the millennium development goals (MDGs), there is at least some progress being achieved and that indeed the MDGs will be met or at least be close to being met. What does this data contribute to our subject matter? This article argues that the data confirms that health desperation in Africa is a very serious reality. What is captured is merely the tip of the mountain, while the broader base is less navigated.

Therefore, for the purposes of our current writing project, we wish to state that health is an important need of humanity which must not be approached in a wishy-washy way. Instead, it should be approached with seriousness that operates with proper reports and measuring validity (Knäuper and Turner 2003). Classical philosophers Plato and Aristotle in their time labored with the importance of health by demanding proper understanding. They are quoted to have drawn an analogy between a "good man" and a "healthy man," as the British philosopher Richard M. Hare rightly argues:

> Philosophers, at least since Plato and Aristotle, have used what may be called the medical analogy when discussing morality; they have claimed that expressions such as "good man" behave in some ways like the expression "healthy man," and that if we have no difficulty in applying the latter, we should have no more difficulty in applying the former. (Hare 1986:174)

We argue that health and subsequently healing is important for humanity and this is confirmed by the fact that socio-political scientists, economists, philosophers and historians all in their respective field address health issues. From all these different angles researchers attest to the fact that health issues are at the core of human existence. If we legitimately state this obvious reality, then the remaining question is whether or not we may argue for the same in a religious context or from a religious context. How important is health and healing for religion and the Bible?

The history of religion and the Bible contain many statements and people who were associated with healing. These healing stories take on several forms of mediation involving the transcendent, human worlds and the

Part 3: THEOLOGICAL REFLECTION

use of matter to bring out restoration. To this I would add that healing and subsequent wellbeing builds bridges between the supreme being and humankind so as to address some fundamental needs which could be health, relationship, water and food, to mention but a few. A variety of titles are applied to describe the important healer figure or person who administers healing.

Philosophical theologian Brian Hebblethwaite (1991:354) argues that:

> Medicine-men, priests, gurus, prophets, sacred kings, avatars and founders of great religions are all in different ways believed to effect some, more or less temporary, bridging the gap between the transcendent, however it is conceived, and ignorant and sinful man.

He further argues that:

> In the religion of the Hebrew Bible, prophets, priests, judges and kings all mediate, as do the Law and the sacrificial cult themselves, between the holy God of Israel and his wayward chosen people. They make known the will of God, proclaim the judgment and the mercy of God and represent God to the people and the people to God (354).

In the above alluded-to statements, mediation is cardinal not only for salvation, but also for normal relationships. The good creation stories where God created everything, evaluated it and concluded that all was good, are eclipsed by the tragic rebellion of humankind against the will of God. That rebellion, which created a steep gap between the Creator and the created, led to other human rebellions and conflicts. Prominent among such rebellions are those of Adam versus Eve (Gen 3), Cain versus Abel (Gen 4), and the adulterous and wicked angels versus the Creator (Gen 6), to mention but a few. These broken relationships grew from bad to worse as humankind increased on the face of the earth. The situation became so much worse that in anticipating the coming of the dreadful day of the LORD (Joel 2:31; Obad 15) the climax of the prophetic tradition points to the Creator's profound yearning for a mediator. The fundamental questions: "Whom shall I send? And who will go for us?" (Isa 6:8), and the charge: "Go and tell this people" (Isa 6:9) have been a subject of reflection for several generations. God is Himself seeking to appoint the mediator to bridge the gap between Him and his estranged people. In other words, the prophetic tradition points to a great hope that the broken relationship will be mended and healed through the services of the mediator.

While we acknowledge the importance of pursuing further probing questions on the above-cited texts and how they were read in context and how we should read them in our postmodern context, we choose to submit that these fundamental questions lead to the messianic hope. The messianic figure does not bridge the gap in a theoretical manner but effectually brings healing in peoples' lives. Such healing is in many ways all-encompassing, affecting the moral, social, spiritual and physical facets of life.

In this regard, we agree with Hebblethwaite (1983:354) when he states that:

> It is a cardinal principle of the NT religion that all these mediatorial roles were taken over and exercised with finality and permanence by Jesus Christ. He is the "one mediator between God and men, Christ Jesus, himself man, who sacrificed himself to win freedom for all humankind." (1 Tim 2:5; see also Heb 9:15; 12:24).

We observe that the above statements are founded on the firm belief that the greatest crisis in the history of humankind and the greatest human need for wellbeing is resolved through the mediatorial qualities and ministry of Jesus Christ. He has rebuilt the broken bridge and mended and healed the broken relationship between the Creator and the created. Jesus's mediating ministry brings about the ideal biblical *shalom*, an all encompassing peace that affects so many aspects of human life and living as we explore further.

Implications of Confessing Jesus as Healer

As we have mentioned before, healing as a form of mediation is a peacemaking concept and in this article we argue that it is actually a peacemaking way of life. It is introduced where relationships are threatened and broken, giving way to conflicts and suffering that have become the order of the day. This is a situation that forms the realities of the Bible and our African contexts.

The theologian Alfred J. Poirier (2006:185) contends that:

> From Genesis 3 to Revelation 21, the Bible is a book abounding with conflict—man against God, God against man, man against man. But the Bible is more. The Bible is God's special revelation of his reconciler. It is the good news of God's promise of a

Part 3: THEOLOGICAL REFLECTION

> Mediator—the coming Prince of Peace. The story of redemption is a story of reconciliation, and that reconciliation is about assisted peacemaking. Redemption calls for divine action; we cannot save or reconcile ourselves. Reconciliation demands another. Reconciliation requires the Messiah as Mediator.

There are a number of issues contained in the above quotation that are relevant to our subject matter. Not only does the Bible abound with conflict and agony, but, much more so, so does our own African continent. As mentioned above, on the one hand, the African continent is one place in the world today where many people worship and pray to the triune God. The Africans demonstrate a lot of commitment by their long and involving service and doing so much with little. To illustrate this claim, one could allude to the fact that many churches in Africa meet their operational costs without endowments which might be relied upon elsewhere. Christianity has greatly outgrown the missionary era; people spend countless more hours at places of worship in Africa than do descendants of the missionary enterprise in their own countries. Yet on the other hand, the paradox, or seemingly contradictory reality, is that there are more hardships and agonies today in Africa than there were in the missionary and colonial era. Some of these hardships and agonies are born out of conflicts based on land, extractive minerals, crude oil, ethnicity, religious beliefs and affiliation, political beliefs and affiliation, to mention but a few. Mention should be made that the above contrast does not in any way suggest that continents and countries that sent out colonialists and missionaries are now flourishing with milk and honey. Some of them may be facing serious hardships which should be recognized. The point of this article is that, overall, African realities are agonizing and complex as the continent remains vulnerable.

Perhaps one lesson to learn from Poirier, quoted above, is that the African continent cannot save or reconcile herself, but needs "another." We can qualify that "another" may not necessarily be a stranger but one of a different type even from within a wider context, one with a healing attitude and qualities and who comes with a different attitude and frame of mind. This means that Africa needs gospel proclamation that transcends the crisis of the moment, a gospel proclamation that will not only plant churches but will also nurture the existing Church and equip it to endure in faith amidst tragedies so that when caught up at the horns of a dilemma, a choice to be obedient to the triune God may be sustained.

African cultures always value the role of healing mediation. In many African cultures, people seek mediation of counselors (*ankhoswe*) in marriage as a form of preventive cure of possible future brokenness. Further, the services of the medicine wo/man (*sing'anga*) when life is threatened. or even of ancestors for general wellbeing, form an inseparable aspect of African life. J. W. M. van Breugel (2001:233) writes about the Chewa people:

> For the Chewa people, illness and death are rarely due to natural causes but to spirits or enemies. It is the task of the diviner (ng'anga) to indicate who caused or sent illness or death. The diviner holds a very important position in Chewa society because he is the only man who can interpret by means of his lots (ula) the will of the spirits of the dead. These mizimu (spirits) are believed to send misfortune in order to warn or to punish their living descendants. The interpretation by the diviner is essential to ascertain what the mizimu want to convey.

For the purposes of our subject matter, what is worthy of noting is the importance of mediation ascribed to the medicine wo/man (*sing'anga* or *ng'anga*) as a healing figure. The conflict between the living and the invisible realities is healed through mediation. What is of importance is that the healing figure seems to discharge functions from some power source beyond. In such a situation, the end justifies the means, which means that methodology becomes less important. In societies where access to such facilities is restricted, as is the case in faith societies, the night and its darkness become allies. The medicine wo/man is approached during the time when the faith community leadership is asleep. We see that in Africa there are many forms of overnight healing vigils. If they will gossip over my concoction during the day, I will go during the night. So seems to be unwritten philosophy of many Africans. In this setting, the Johannine narrative involving Nicodemus seeking the services of Jesus in the night is read with admiration (John 3:1–21). With these eyes, the hero is not Jesus but Nicodemus, the wise one. Though one rightfully questions the interpretation of the narrative, the message is clear that the need for wellbeing is more important than the procedures and prestige people publicly observe. Where health is concerned, all means are worth trying.

When does Jesus become a real hero in the lives of many African people? Already early in the gospel narratives Jesus established himself as the conqueror or power figure when he overcame Satan during the temptation in the desert. The confrontation that saw Jesus emerge victorious took place early in the narratives. Subsequent exorcisms and acts of healing are a result of that resolution.

To signal the proximity and presence of God's rule in the world, Jesus exorcised. He also healed leprosy and various illnesses, healed hunger by feeding multitudes, and restored sight and hearing, to mention but a few healing signs of Jesus.

Reading these healing narratives with African eyes does not only appreciate the fact that these powerful acts display God's reign in the world, but also appreciates that Jesus is the change agent who transforms people by employing superior power to render healing to humanity. In societies where people face massive poverty and live on less than one American dollar per day, where health infrastructure and systems have collapsed due to corruption, in societies ravaged by HIV/AIDS related diseases and other perennial illnesses and cultural vandalism due to dirty politics, what Jesus is welcomed? This is one of the key questions that the reader should bear in mind as we move towards concluding our writing.

Conclusion

In concluding this brief study that aims at stimulating further research that can contribute to an African Christology which we contend is of critical necessity, the following propositions are offered towards the quest for an African Christology:

- Jesus is the Mediator according to the fulfilled prophetic tradition and primarily he bridges the gap between the Creator and the created. The greatest conflict, which is the one between God and humans, is, through the mediatorial services of Jesus Christ, healed. Thereby, fear, sin and death are transformed into love and relationship.

- A Jesus who is narrowly concerned about the saving of the soul for the future but neglects the holistic issues of life, including incumbent wellbeing, is not welcome in Africa, as we argue. The Jesus for Africa should always transcend the emotional crisis of the moment. He should transform life beyond the revival rally, to continue as the believer faces daunting questions of trusting God in all circumstances both now and for eternity.

- Confessing Jesus as healer has implications for Christianity and the world we live in today. To be Christian is to embody Christ Jesus in daily living, and confessing Jesus as the Healer means that wellbeing is not a right of the privileged few but a way of living for all. Christianity must get concerned whenever life is endangered because endangered life leads to vulnerability which is an impediment to shalom as a gift of our triune God. When wellbeing is threatened, Christians ought not ask why they should be involved, but why they should not be involved, because agony challenges the very core of the identity of their savior and themselves.

- No human society can save or reconcile itself no matter how sophisticated that society becomes. There is a place for using the services of "another," or for "assisted peacemaking," which can only be done by one or more objective outside persons having an audience with the estranged parties and then finding appropriate possible solutions (Sande 2004:21–27).

- Christianity as a manifestation of the Kingdom has no option but to administer healing in all of its possible forms. Ministers, missionaries, teachers, preachers, priests, seminarians and all in Christian ministry are not worth their salt if they neglect wellbeing.

- In search of healing, humanity volunteers everything out of desperation. Desperate people manifest desperate behaviors, and this is what proponents of the prosperity gospel have discovered and have learned to take advantage of.

- Arm-chair criticism of the prosperity gospel is neither sufficient nor necessary. Sub-Saharan average citizenry are under the siege of many tragedies and health failures, a situation that renders them vulnerable and desperate. Anything that appears to work stands for something concrete that our people desperately need. Therefore, if there is anything wrong with the prosperity gospel as a healing approach, then alternatives must be put in place. If they are not handling it well, then concerned minds should handle it well; otherwise it is honorable to forever keep their peace.

- The Church of the future and the future of the Church, at least from an African perspective, require addressing wellbeing issues here and now, too, if the church's presence as a healing community is to be noticed and valued.

Part 3: THEOLOGICAL REFLECTION

Bibliography

Hare, R. M. 1986. "Health." *Journal of Medical Ethics* 12, no. 4:174–81.

Hebblethwaite, A. 1983. "Mediator." In A. Richardson and J. Bowden, eds. *The Westminster Dictionary of Christian Theology*, 354–55. Philadelphia: The Westminster Press.

Jenkins, P. 2002. *The Next Christendom: The Coming of Global Christianity*. Oxford: Oxford University Press.

Knäuper, B., and P. A. Turner. 2003. "Measuring Health: Improving the Validity of Health Assessment." *Quality of Life Research* 12:81–89.

Poirier, A. 2006. *The Peacemaking Pastor: A Biblical Guide to Resolving Church Conflict*. Grand Rapids, MI: Baker.

Sande, K. 2004. *The Peacemaker: A Biblical Guide to Resolving Personal Conflict*. Grand Rapids, MI: Baker.

Van Breugel, J. M. W. 2001. *Chewa Traditional Religion*. Blantyre: CLAIM.

World Health Organization. 2012. "World Health Statistics 2012." *World Health Organization* [online]. Available at: http://www.who.int/gho/publications/world_health_statistics/2012/en/.

5

Dialoguing at "Mphala"

A Conversation on Faith between John Calvin and Proponents of the Prosperity Gospel

LAMECK BANDA

"FAITH" SEEMS TO BE a simple and straightforward word. However, a further analysis shows that it is one of the many terms which receive various definitions. A close look at the biblical perspective reveals a plurality of meanings of "faith."[1] In some instances "faith" is understood simply as "belief," "trust," or "hope." In others it is having the right attitude to God, or a spirit of trustfulness in a person of faith. From a Reformed perspective, faith would mean a situation where one abandons all trust in one's own resources. Instead, s/he casts him/herself unreservedly on God's care and mercy. Morris (1996:360) gives a concise Trinitarian understanding of faith: "Faith means laying hold on the promises of God in Christ, relying entirely on the finished work of Christ for salvation, and on the power

---

1. The aim of this article is not to give a detailed analysis of the biblical perspective of "faith," but rather to stress the fact that one's perspective influences the conceptualization of "faith," and if not checked it could possibly be in tension with other people's perspectives.

Part 3: THEOLOGICAL REFLECTION

of the indwelling Holy Spirit of God for daily strength." Faith, in the end, is complete reliance on and full obedience to the triune God.

Unfortunately, due to different perspectives on the understanding of faith, a tension has been created between the Reformed tradition[2] and the prosperity gospel movement, and this tension continues to escalate. On one hand, the Reformed tradition seems to be more theocentric in its understanding of faith. God stands out as the ultimate actor in the bestowing of faith to humanity, and humanity, in return, answers in faith to what God has done. On the other hand, the prosperity gospel movement appears to be more anthropocentric in its conceptualization of faith. Humanity is primarily the architect of faith, where a person takes the initiative and applies one's efforts in the exercise of faith. This scenario obviously has created an ever-increasing tension between the two conceptualizations of faith. The crucial question, then, is: how can the two perspectives link so as to possibly enhance harmony in the body of Christ?

In order to uphold a dialogical approach (a route of conversation, chatting, and discussing where you create an environment for exchange of ideas, and open channels for communication) as a way of reducing the tension and bringing linkage between the two conceptualizations of faith, the article proposes and upholds the Chewa[3] concept of "mphala."[4] The "mphala" concept is justifiable because of three key attributes: firstly, it is social in nature, in that it embraces all participants at a gathering for dialogue; secondly, it is biblically based in that it articulates the "body of Christ" metaphor of the church as given in 1 Corinthians 12:12–30; and, thirdly, it is theologically sound in that the Trinitarian relational and *perichoresis* views are upheld. The article emphatically dispels both passivism and confrontational approaches because they do great harm to the body of Christ; hence, the need to work for dialogue.

---

2. This article discusses John Calvin's conceptualization of faith: hence, Calvin acts as a representative of the Reformed tradition.

3. "Chewa" is the researchers tribe and mother-tongue language, mainly situated in the Eastern region of Zambia.

4. The word "mphala" has a number of meanings: (a) a place for socialising; (b) a house for unmarried boys—all the bachelors in a family are traditionally confined to a "mphala"; and (c) a local court in a village where legal matters and cases are communally presided over and decided on. For the sake of this article, the first meaning takes prominence although allusion to the second and third meanings is made in passing. In the contemporary technological world, a "mphala" would be similar to Facebook, which provides a space for social networking. The article interprets the social networking as dialogue which takes place at "mphala" or on Facebook.

Theocentric Dimension: John Calvin's Thought on Faith

The Reformed tradition is, in general terms, considered to be a movement that focuses on a spiritual renewal of the faith and mission of the church. It is a theological tradition "that emerged from the work of John Calvin and other reformers such as Huldrych Zwingli and Heinrich Bullinger in contrast to Lutheranism and Anabaptism in the sixteenth century" (McKim 1996:234). Although Calvin stands out as one of the key proponents of the Reformed tradition, there were other reformers who prominently sought to reform the church, its theology and practices. All these sought to reform the Roman Catholic Church during the sixteenth-century Reformation. In this article, however, we focus on John Calvin's work, especially his understanding of faith. For a moment, let us briefly understand who Calvin was and his main theological motifs.

John Calvin was born in the farm town of Noyon on 10 July 1509 (McKim 2004:3). The town was situated in Picardy, in Northern France, a farm country marked by strong religious and ecclesiastical ties. McKim further informs us that Calvin's father was a financial administrator of the cathedral chapter of Noyon. His mother, who died early, was a humble woman who had zeal for making religious pilgrimages. Calvin studied law and theology, and became so influential that his theology was widely accepted and practiced. The main motif in Calvin's theology is the *knowledge of God* and of ourselves. He emphasized this mainly in the Institutes. He states, "Nearly all the wisdom we posses, that is to say, true and sound wisdom, consists of two parts: the knowledge of God and of ourselves, But, while joined by many bonds, which one precedes and brings forth the other is not easy to discern" (Inst. I.i.1). In the motif on the knowledge of God Calvin elaborates two major headings, the knowledge of God the Creator and the knowledge of God the Redeemer (McKim 2004:78). Faith is about and focuses on God whom we know as our Creator and the Redeemer of humankind. Therefore, the discussion on faith revolves around the main motif of Calvin's theology.

What then, is the outlook of Calvin's conceptualization of faith? Perhaps it is appropriate at the onset to note that Calvin situates the discussion of faith in the context of the way humanity receives the grace of Christ. This grace has benefits for us and is effectual for those that receive it. It is within this context that faith is defined and explained in detail. According to Calvin, faith is "a firm and certain knowledge of God's benevolence towards us, founded upon the truth of the freely given promise in Christ, both revealed

Part 3: THEOLOGICAL REFLECTION

to our minds and sealed upon our hearts through the Holy Spirit" (Inst. III. ii.7). From this definition we can deduce the theological meaning of faith as Calvin understands it.

In Calvin's view, faith emanates from God's promise of grace in Christ. It is not something that originates from the fallible and finite human mind; it is God who works out faith in human beings, which they in turn express as a response to God, the author and perfector of that faith. Faith does not base itself on pious ignorance where you understand nothing, provided that you only submit your feelings obediently to the church. Faith rests on the knowledge not only of God, but also of divine will (Inst. III.ii.14). It consists in understanding who God is in his being, and understanding his desire for our lives as creatures. Calvin further states that faith rests upon God's word (Inst. III.ii.13;21;31;33-37). This word of God is like a mirror in which faith may contemplate who God really is as revealed to humankind. From the word of God we tend to rightly perceive the nature of God, and to develop in ourselves the knowledge of God's will toward us. This is made possible by the effectual working of the Holy Spirit.

In short, we may think of Calvin's conceptualization of faith as Trinitarian in nature. To believe is to have a firm and certain knowledge of the triune God. The triune God exercises God's benevolence towards us. God's in-breaking and sacrificial love graciously meets us for relationship and fellowship with God. The death and resurrection of Jesus Christ makes this action by God a reality in our lives. Through the death of Jesus Christ our death to sinful nature is attained, and through the resurrection of Jesus Christ our resurrection to new life is assured. Furthermore, the knowledge of God's benevolence in the death and resurrection of Jesus Christ is not only revealed to our minds, but also is sealed upon our hearts by the Holy Spirit. This is what we can affirm as the basis of our salvation and the assurance of eternal life. The triune God shares Himself with humanity because God is a relational being who wants to be in communion with us for eternal fellowship. Real faith does not neglect God's relationality as our anchor of the Christian faith.

Calvin thinks of faith as that which grants hope (Inst. III.ii.15-16). It is not a dead and passive faith which has no meaning and purposeful goal. The knowledge of faith consists in the assurance of hope in the triune God. Faith requires full and firm certainty, the sure confidence in the divine benevolence and salvation. The certainty of faith is that the promises of mercy that God offers are true, and we make them ours by inwardly embracing them. Faith, in this sense, sustains the hearts of the believers amidst the struggle against temptation and all the challenges of life we experience each day (Inst. III.ii.17–18). In other words, faith arouses hope—the expectation of those things which faith has believed to have been truly promised by God (Inst. III.ii.29–30;32). Faith believes God to be true, and hope awaits the time when this truth shall be manifested. Faith and hope depend on each other in a sense: inasmuch as faith is the foundation upon which hope rests, hope also nourishes and sustains faith. You cannot hope for something you do not believe in; you believe in something in which you have hope. So, faith and hope go hand in hand, and both of them have the same foundation: God's mercy or grace, not the good works one may perform (Inst. III.iii.41–43).

Faith and hope are based on the grace of God, manifested in the sacrificial work of Jesus Christ, which is sustained by the Holy Spirit. But, then, for what purpose is this gracious act of God? It is true that we have faith in God to enjoy everlasting relationship with our Creator. Beyond this communion with God there is need for extended communion with other people and the rest of creation. Therefore, we answer to the grace of God in faith by doing good works, not to merit eternal life but as our gratitude for God's mercy on us. According to Calvin, this expression of gratitude for God's mercy is love or charity. There is a link, therefore, between faith and charity. In response to God's grace, faith kindles in us a love for God and others. Listen to Calvin's own strong words: "For the teaching of the schoolmen, that love is prior to faith and hope, is mere madness; for it is faith alone that first engenders love in us" (Inst. III.iii.41). Here, Calvin is castigating the idea that good works merit one's salvation. His point is threefold: firstly, you cannot have forgiveness of sins apart from God's mercy; secondly, you cannot have a good work at all unless God gives it to you; and thirdly, you cannot merit eternal life by any works unless that is also given freely. In short, forgiveness of sins, good works and eternal life are granted by God. Therefore, our good works—works of charity—are actually a response to what God has already done, is doing, and continues to do in us through his grace in Jesus Christ and the empowerment of the Holy Spirit.

Part 3: THEOLOGICAL REFLECTION

Anthropocentric Dimension: The Prosperity Gospel View of Faith

The genesis of the prosperity gospel took place in the 1940s. A Wikipedia (2013) article on "Prosperity theology" further explains that it was during the Post-war healing revivals that the prosperity gospel first came to prominence in the United States. Its teaching later became prominent in the so called "Word of Faith" movement and in the televangelism of the 1980s. Later, in the 1990s and 2000s, it was adopted by influential leaders in the Charismatic movements and promoted by Christian missionaries throughout the world. This led to the establishment of mega-churches. These churches are in most cases non-denominational and usually directed by a sole pastor or leader, although some have developed multi-church networks that bear similarities to denominations (Wikipedia 2013). According to *Faith and Finance* founder "Tim" (2011), such churches typically set aside extended time to teach about giving and request donations from the congregation, encouraging positive speech and faith. Prosperity churches often teach about "financial responsibility." This is because the prosperity movement teaches that God wants Christians to be prosperous financially, physically, spiritually, and in every other aspect of life.

The prosperity gospel is also known by different names which include terms such as "Positive Confession," "Word-Faith" or "Word of Faith" theology, the "Health and Wealth gospel," "Name It and Claim It," and "Prosperity Teaching" or "Prosperity Theology." These terms define what this movement is all about. Joel Osteen is known for his open-arms, positive-thinking, God-wants-to-bless-you approach to Christianity, which has actually earned him a loyal and large following of millions worldwide and the largest and fastest growing church in United States. Michelle A. Vu (2012), a *Christian Post* reporter, posed a question to Osteen concerning the nature of the prosperity gospel. His response explains a lot about the movement:

> *Michelle*: Do you consider yourself a preacher of the prosperity gospel? Is it heresy?
>
> *Osteen*: You know, I don't consider myself a . . . I don't really know what the prosperity gospel is. The way I define it is that I believe God wants you to prosper in your health, in your family, in your relationships, in your business, and in your career. So I do . . . if that is the prosperity gospel, then I do believe that. I don't believe we are supposed to go through life defeated and not having enough money to pay our bills or send our kids to college.

From Osteen's response one would define prosperity gospel as a Christian religious doctrine which claims the Bible teaches that financial blessing is the will of God for Christians (Wikipedia 2013). In other words, the doctrine teaches that faith, positive speech, and donations to Christian ministries will increase one's material wealth.

Preachers of the prosperity gospel have influenced millions of eager listeners who are desperate to hear the promising message of the prosperity gospel. Hence, the movement has grown worldwide. Gary E. Gilley (1999) explains that today the prosperity gospel movement is "the fastest growing segment of professing Christianity." This growth is at least partially due to the massive amounts of money the leaders are able to extract from the faithful. The influx of cash allows for huge buildings and extensive ministries, and wide exposure on television, which translates into numerical growth. One interesting factor about the growth of this movement is that it is mainly significant among the poor and middle class of the Third World, and also outside the mainstream churches. One of the reasons for this scenario is that the poor of impoverished countries often find the doctrine of prosperity gospel more appealing than that of the mainline churches because of the poor's economic powerlessness and the prosperity gospel's emphasis on miracles. This is also why the prosperity gospel is spreading rapidly across sub-Saharan Africa.

The main proponents of prosperity gospel theology include Kenneth Hagin, Kenneth Copeland, Benny Hinn, Frederick K. C. Price, John Avanzini, Robert Tilton, Marilyn Hickey, David Yonggi Cho, Charles Capps, Jerry Savelle, Morris Cerullo, Paul and Jan Crouch, and many others (Gilley 1999). Some of the prominent names in Africa include Chris Oyakhilome and Apostle Simon Mokoena (Van der Watt forthcoming). What is noticeable about the lifestyle of these personalities is that they are wearing fancy suits, driving posh cars, living a luxurious life, and amassing wealth. They also assure their followers that they, too, can attain this, if only they apply certain principles. Together with their followers, they claim to base their faith and practices on the Word of God, and yet one would notice that much emphasis is on experiences and feelings.

Much has been discussed concerning the phenomenon and proponents of prosperity gospel. Now, how does the prosperity gospel movement conceptualize faith? The main thrust of this movement of faith is that God's desire is to see the material, spiritual, and physical prosperity of his people. "To become prosperous, all one has to do is believe, receive, and act upon

Part 3: THEOLOGICAL REFLECTION

God's promised prosperity" (McKnight 2009). Brace (2000) adds that in prosperity gospel theology "faith . . . becomes something which requires God to give us everything we want, whether it is ever-radiant health, financial affluence or that spectacular gift to impress fellow-believers! If we do our bit, then God *must* act!" God must act immediately, here and now. Therefore, as Professor in Christian ethics David Jones (1998) rightly notes, in this movement faith is not a theocentric act of personal will, or simple trust in God; but rather an anthropocentric spiritual force which is directed at God. In a sense, words are a creative force, with the power of influencing both the physical and the spiritual world (Hein 2004). What you say determines everything that happens to you. For this reason, the things you say must all be stated positively and without wavering. Then God is *required* to answer (Biblical Discernment Ministries 1996).

In a nutshell, faith is a formula by which you manipulate God according to laws that govern the universe. It is about "positive confession."[5] "You can be rich, healthy and trouble free. Jesus was rich and God wants you to be rich" (Sherrell 1997). What it requires is faith. Gilley (1999) testifies that "faith works like a mighty power or force. Through faith, we can obtain anything we want—health, wealth, success, whatever." However, this force is only released through the spoken word (Soto 2003). As we speak the words of faith, power is discharged to accomplish our desires.

Having explained faith according to the prosperity gospel, it is worthy to briefly mention the key doctrinal pillars in relationship to the subject at hand. Faith in prosperity gospel theology encompasses the following doctrinal pillars:

Faith as spoken word (rhematology). This is a theology which stresses the inherent power of words and thoughts (Watchman Fellowship 2000). Brace (2003a) explains, "According to this teaching, we ourselves have tremendous dynamic power to force God to act, just as long as we are utterly positive."

Faith for health. This is the belief that according to God's plan believers are never sick and never die prematurely (Hein 2004). In other words, the prosperity gospel teaches that a believer cannot fall sick, on account of God's great love and mercy.

---

5. By "positive confession" here, the meaning does not lie in one's belief in a set of theological teachings or doctrines. For the prosperity gospel the meaning lies in positive pronouncement and attitude towards what one wants to achieve. In this case, it refers to making a positive pronouncement and having a positive attitude towards the desired good health and wealth.

Faith for wealth. This is a central tenet of the prosperity gospel which states that God wills the financial prosperity of every Christian (Hein 2004). If a believer lives in poverty, s/he is living outside God's intended will. Every believer must realize that it is God's will for him/her to prosper; all it requires is faith in this God who prospers every believer. Since believers are God's children, they should always be first class and the best in all that they do, and in prosperity.

It is clear the prosperity gospel teaches that God used the word to bring everything into existence. Believers, too, have the potential, through faith, to bring good health and prosperity into reality. To be sick and in debt only shows a lack of faith.

Quest for Linkage: Dialogue at "Mphala"

So far we have discussed how the Reformed tradition (here represented by John Calvin) and the prosperity gospel movement each conceptualize faith. The question of how the two conceptualizations can link in order to enhance harmony still remains. The two perspectives have three approaches to take. The first is a *passivism approach*: an unenthusiastic, inert and inactive route where each of them accepts the status quo and lets the other go its own way—a kind of "standoff" situation. This, in the end, does not solve any problem at all because there is no linkage between the two, thereby letting the tension continue to grow. The second is a *confrontational approach*: an argumentative, antagonistic and aggressive route where each of the two opts to attack the other with the view of championing their own traditional view on faith. This approach obviously may worsen the situation, depending on the perspective from which one takes this approach. In short, the first two options are problematic in that neither does anything to resolve the tension. A more appropriate approach would be a *dialogical approach*: a conversational, chatting and discussing route where you open channels of communication and create an environment for exchanging ideas. In this article, therefore, a "mphala" concept is considered as an appropriate approach toward establishing linkage between the two conceptualizations.

The "mphala" concept is preferred in bringing and enhancing dialogue between the two perspectives on faith because of its nature. A "mphala" is a forum for having meaningful communication, sharing (a give-and-take situation), and listening to and respecting other peoples' views. Everyone in a "mphala" is always available and willing to participate in an open

Part 3: THEOLOGICAL REFLECTION

dialogue. It is a social network where everyone participates in the chats and discussions on issues that concern members of the network. We now proceed to look at why the "mphala" is an appropriate option for bringing linkage between the two conceptualizations on faith.

First of all, the "mphala" concept is *social in nature,* in that it embraces all participants at a gathering for dialogue. At "mphala" people dialogue freely: in a meaningful dialogue everyone is at liberty to express personal opinions. No one's views are suppressed. Where people enter into a dialogue there is also solidarity and justice for all. Furthermore, where people experience real dialogue there is a sense of unhindered and open communion in solidarity with one another. Therefore, we would confidently state that at "mphala" there is a social aspect of wholeheartedly embracing one another.

Theologians Judith Gundry-Volf and Miroslav Volf give theological views which could be helpful for us to understand the solidarity that is characterized by embrace of the other. Gundry-Volf focuses on the encounters of Jesus with the Samaritan woman in John 4:1–42 and the Syrophoenician woman in Mark 7:24–30 and Matthew 15:21–28, which are both about crossing boundaries of mission. Volf's essay, "Exclusion and Embrace" (Volf 1997a:11), aims at suggesting new theological categories in order to help the church deal with conflicts between cultures. Both theologians call for opening ourselves to the Spirit of God, the Spirit of mercy, justice, and truth; and for the healing of our world by embracing "others" as we remain true to ourselves (Volf 1997a:11). In other words, both theologians are guided by the notion of "embrace" in their theological and missiological reflection. Volf (1997a:10) explains that "embrace stands for reaching out to "others" and finding a place *within ourselves as individuals and cultures for "other" while still remaining ourselves.*" Embracing means while still maintaining our identity we open doors for people other than ourselves, and who are different from us, so that they, too, may find a room within ourselves. Embrace, according to Volf (1997b:58), always involves a double movement: (a) *aperture*—opening arms to create space for others, as a sign of discontent at being myself only and of desire to include the others. It is also a gesture showing that the others are invited in and should feel at home with me and should know that, on some level, they belong to me; and (b) *closure*—gently closing my arms around the others so as to tell them that I do not want to be without them in their otherness.

Embrace is a social understanding of reconciliation expressed at "mphala" which demonstrates true solidarity and dialogue for mutual and harmonious life in the community. No one is sidelined, because once everyone is embraced. What follows is interrelationship, and a mutual sharing of life that emanates from the true sense of being in a community.

The other reason why the "mphala" is an appropriate option is that it fleshes out biblical concepts, articulating the "body of Christ" metaphor of the church as given in 1 Corinthians 12:12–31. The church as the "body of Christ" is "a communion of persons who in all of their differences from each other form one body" (Horton 2011:736). The "mphala" exemplifies the "body of Christ" metaphor in that it is, as well, a communion of persons who, despite having different backgrounds and interests, form one community for the ultimate common purpose of harmonious existence. In 1 Corinthians 12:12–31 Paul articulates the organic image of the church as a body whose head is Christ (Migliore 1991:191). The church is a community which participates in one Lord, one Spirit, one baptism, and thus becomes one "body of Christ." Migliore further explains that the metaphor of the "body of Christ" conveys the mutual dependence of all the members of the community on one another, their variety of gifts which are for the enrichment and edification of the whole community, and the common dependence of all members of the body on the one head, who is Christ. This is the epitome of unity in diversity.

The "mphala" concept seeks to covey this same message of interdependence and co-existence regardless of the individual community members' unique giftings and differences. Where the "mphala" lifestyle is promoted, each member depends on the others for new and progressive ideas, for skills and the overall up-building of the community. Because every participant in the "mphala" is mindful that s/he is connected to the others in the community, meaningful dialogue takes place. Everyone pays attention to the others with the intention to listen and learn from what others contribute to the dialogue. At this point, I am even tempted not to call it "dialogue" anymore because dialogue is about a discussion of two people or groups. At "mphala" we see what one would term as "multi-logue," if at all we have such a term in the English language, or "conversation." But for now we will stick to "dialogue" since our aim is to bring linkage between the Reformed tradition and the prosperity gospel movement on their view of faith.

The "mphala" concept is appropriate for the linkage of the Reformed tradition and the prosperity gospel movement because it is *theologically sound*, in that the Trinitarian values of relationship and *perichoresis* are upheld. The "mphala" concept portrays the essence and life in the Trinity.

Part 3: THEOLOGICAL REFLECTION

According to Migliore (1991:67) the depth grammar of Trinitarian faith is the "grammar of wondrous divine love that freely gives of itself to others and creates community, mutuality, and shared life. God creates and relates to the world this way because this is the way God is eternally God." From this essence of God as love, flows personal life in relationship, community existence and self-giving love. God establishes and maintains community (1991:69), in which the deepest relationship of God Himself in three persons is to indwell each other (*perichoresis*). They create room for and are hospitable to each other, which shows that the members of the Godhead live and act in one accord.

There is no room for individualism (centeredness on the individual at the expense of life for the wellbeing of the community) and segregation in "mphala." Love is demonstrated through the interrelatedness of all individuals in the community. The African communal existence, coupled with a sharing of love and life, can be recipes for mutual and harmonious existence that can bring a linkage between differing groups. For this reason, the "mphala" concept is helpful in bringing the Reformed tradition and the prosperity gospel movement together for dialogue.

Having analyzed the nature of the "mphala" concept above, it is vital to point out specific lessons to take away, from which the two opposing traditions can learn. Here I just highlight key areas of importance to take note of if we are at all to see harmony between the Reformed tradition and the prosperity gospel movement. These areas could also be treated as points of contact and dialogue between the two perspectives.

First, there is need to bear in mind a *balanced understanding of God*. On one hand we understand God as supreme, sovereign, incomprehensible and all-powerful. With this in mind we are limited and compelled to avoid any form of manipulation of this God because we are mere fallible and finite creatures in God's hands. On the other hand, the God we believe in is also a relational, loving, merciful and caring God. This in itself gives us confidence to approach God in humility, joy and assurance for God's blessings in health and wealth. Hence, each of the two traditions needs to reflect on whether it might possibly be holding on to either an abstract view of God or a manipulation and belittling of God.

Second, there is need to pay attention to the *message of Scripture*. A holistic and contextual reading and interpretation of scripture is required for its appropriate application to the contemporary scenario. When this broad view of scripture is taken seriously, faith is properly understood in a wider context. The message of scripture should help members of the Reformed tradition to view faith in practical and concrete terms; while for the prosperity gospel movement, the scriptural message needs to assist in viewing faith not as something propelled by human effort, but as an act of God which requires a response in love, obedience, commitment and service.

Third, there is a need to understand *God's will and plans*. God fulfils his will and plans with or without human faith. God can still heal and make a person prosper regardless of the amount of faith one has. Furthermore, God is not obliged to heal or prosper anyone. In his goodness God graciously heals and makes one prosper. This needs to be taken seriously by the prosperity gospel movement; there is a need to realize that healing and any form of wealth come from God according to God's will and plans. A balance should also be struck from the side of the Reformed tradition: God's will and plans should not be limited by an avoidance to act upon what we believe to be God's will and plans.

Fourth, there is need for *humility and total dependence on God*. We need to come before God in prayer by adopting what Brace (2005) calls "a vulnerable and humble approach." While we approach God in prayer with confidence, we should also bear in mind that "we are placing a matter before the Creator and Ruler of the very universe and we are directly involving [God] in whatever problem or need we may face." We need to humble ourselves and rely on God to provide healing and bestow prosperity.

Fifth, there is need to provide a *relevant theology to the current context*. It must be able to take the needs of the people seriously by taking the true meaning of faith in the Bible and making it relevant to the situation of the people who experience challenges in life on a daily basis. A good theology is relevant when it addresses social, political, economic, cultural, ecological and spiritual issues that affect people.

Lastly, there is need to practice faith with *personal integrity*. Faith must manifest itself in both private and public moral life. Leaders from both traditions should strive to overcome what someone has called the threefold temptations of pride or power, popularity or success and wealth or greed, and exemplify a life of humility, integrity and simplicity. In both of these traditions there is a need to be aware of the easy temptation to falling into fanciness and luxury at the expense of the ordinary congregants.

Part 3: THEOLOGICAL REFLECTION

Conclusion: A Call for Dialogue

Dialoguing at "mphala" requires both the Reformed tradition and the prosperity gospel movement to have biblically and theologically acceptable conceptualizations of faith. Hence, faith must be defined in a proper biblical and theological context. Brace (2003b) tries to define faith from a biblical and theological premise. He states that faith is "an utterly close walk with a God who has revealed Himself to us; it will constantly tend to manifest itself in a wholehearted trust that God means what he says, even when all appearances might suggest otherwise." This faith is passed on to a believer through the sanctifying work of the Holy Spirit. Faith in the end must be action-oriented, embodying full trust, confidence, and recognition of the sovereignty and jurisdiction of God in all areas of human life.

A biblical and theological understanding of faith would significantly reduce tension between the Reformed tradition and the prosperity gospel movement, in that the focus would not be what I can do, but what God does in and through my life. Dialoguing at "mphala" could be an alternative avenue for sharing insights on faith which have the potential to bring harmony in the body of Christ. Therefore, the Reformed faith and prosperity gospel theology are called upon to open dialogue at "mphala."

Bibliography

Biblical Discernment Ministries. 1996. "Positive Confession/PMA: Prosperity Gospel and the New Age." Rapidnet.com [online]. Available at: http://www.rapidnet.com/~jbeard/bdm/Psychology/posit.htm.

Brace, R. A. 2000. "Signs and Wonders: Don't Believe Every Claim!" UK Apologetics [online]. Available at: http://www.ukapologetics.net/signs.htm.

———. 2003a. "Can Our 'Positive Confession' Force God to Change Course?" UK Apologetics [online]. Available at: http://www.ukapologetics.net/1positive.htm.

———. 2003b. "All about Faith: What Is Faith? What Isn't Faith?" UK Apologetics [online]. Available at: http://www.ukapologetics.net/5faithis.htm.

———. 2005. "Vulnerability of Godly Prayer." UK Apologetics [online]. Available at: http://www.ukapologetics.net/vulnerable.html.

Gilley, G. E. 1999. "The Word of Faith Movement." Rapidnet.com [online]. Available at: http://www.rapidnet.com/~jbeard/bdm/Psychology/char/more/w-f.htm.

Gundry-Volf, J. M. 1997. "Spirit, Mercy, and the 'Other.'" In J. M. Gundry-Volf and M. Volf, *A Spacious Heart: Essays on Identity and Belonging*, 12–32. Harrisburg, PA: Trinity Press International.

Hein, A. 2004. "Positive Confession: A Word-Faith Doctrine." *Apologetics Index* [online]. Available at: http://www.apologeticsindex.org/p/p23.html.

Horton, M. 2011. *The Christian Faith: A Systematic Theology for Pilgrims on the Way.* Grand Rapids, MI: Zondervan.

Watchman Fellowship. 2000. "How the Health and Wealth Gospel Twists Scripture." Watchman.org [online]. Available at: http://www.watchman.org/reltop/health$.htm.

Jones, D. W. 1998. "The Bankruptcy of the Prosperity Gospel: An Exercise in Biblical and Theological Ethics." Bible.org [online]. Available at: http://bible.org/article/bankruptcy-prosperity-gospel-exercise-biblical-and-theological-ethics.

McKim, D. K. 1996. *Westminster Dictionary of Theological Terms.* Louisville: Westminster John Knox.

———. 2004. *The Cambridge Companion to John Calvin.* Cambridge: Cambridge University.

McKnight, S. 2009. "The Problem for the Prosperity Gospel." Beliefnet.com [online]. Available at: http://www.beliefnet.com/Faiths/Christianity/2009/03/The-Problem-for-the-Prosperity-Gospel.aspx.

McNeill, J. T. 1960. *Calvin's Institutes of the Christian Religion.* Vol. 1. Louisville: Westminster John Knox.

Migliore, D. L. 1991. *Faith Seeking Understanding: An Introduction to Christian Theology.* Grand Rapids, MI: Eerdmans.

Morris, L. L. 1996. "Faith." In J. D. Douglas, ed. *New Bible Dictionary,* 357–60. 3rd ed. Leicester: Inter-Varsity.

Paas, S. 2009. *Mtanthauziramawu—Chichewa/Chinyanja to English and English to Chichewa/Chinyanja Dictionary.* Zomba: Kachere.

Sherrell, R. 1997. "Cult or Christianity? World Changers Promises Financial Blessings to the Faithful, but Many Leave Disillusioned." Apologetics Index [online]. Available at: http://www.apologeticsindex.org/d11.html.

Soto, N. 2003. "Is It a Sin to Be Rich or Not?" UK Apologetics [online]. Available at: http://www.ukapologetics.net/08/richornot.htm.

Tim, 2011. "Why the Prosperity Gospel Is Wrong." Faith and Finance [online]. Available at: http://www.faithandfinance.org/2011/10/why-the-prosperity-gospel-is-wrong/.

Van der Watt, G. Forthcoming. "'But the Poor Opted for the Evangelicals!'—Evangelicals, Poverty and Prosperity."

Volf, M. 1997a. In J. M. Gundry-Volf and M. Volf, introduction to *A Spacious Heart: Essays on Identity and Belonging,* 1–11. Harrisburg, PA: Trinity Press International.

———, 1997b. "Exclusion and Embrace: Theological Reflection in the Wake of 'Ethnic cleansing.'" In J. M. Gundry-Volf and M. Volf, *A Spacious Heart: Essays on Identity and Belonging,* 33–60. Harrisburg, PA: Trinity Press International.

Vu, M. A. 2012. "Church and Ministries." *Christian Post* [online]. Available at: http://www.christianpost.com/news/interview-joel-osteen-on-prosperity-gospel-crystal-cathedral-and-jesus-74040/.

Wikipedia. 2013. "Prosperity Theology." Wikipedia [online]. Available at: http://en.wikipedia.org/wiki/Prosperity_theology.

6

The Prosperity Gospel

A Way to Reclaim Dignity?

HERMEN KROESBERGEN

"Do you want better health? Do you want more wealth? This year you will get it. God has prepared a miracle with your name on it. Just believe!" In Zambia on the radio and on television I hear this same message being proclaimed over and over. And it puzzles me. How can people say these kinds of things? Am I misunderstanding them? Do they mean something else? They cannot really be saying what they appear to be saying, can they? So I wonder.

The Ghanaian preacher Mensa Otabil, in *Enjoying the Blessings of Abraham*, claims it is simply not possible "for the person that operates under the blessing of Abraham to get poorer"—just have faith, like Abraham had (quoted in Gifford 1998:81). He refers to the story of Abraham, who had to sacrifice his son Isaac. He obeys God, he has faith, and at the crucial moment God provides a ram to sacrifice. Abraham kept his son, and both became rich. In the same way a believer cannot get poorer. But how can Otabil say this? And, how can people believe it? It appears to be a blatant untruth: many believers will become poorer. Just like many listeners to the radio and television will, and they will become ill this year, and some will die. These preachers seem to be lying—without even hiding it.

I learnt that this message is called the prosperity gospel, and it puzzles me.

A Puzzling Message

Failing to Understand

There are at least two ways in which I fail to understand the prosperity gospel. On the one hand, the message of the prosperity gospel, with its emphasis on this-worldly goods, seems to me to be completely at odds with Christianity: biblically, historically and theologically.

On the other hand, the message of the prosperity gospel seems to me to be simply factually not true. If you say the people will get health and wealth this very year, and many of them become ill, some even die, and many become poorer, it appears to me that you have just lied to the people. What can it mean to say what the prosperity gospel appears to be saying?

Unchristian and Foolish?

I am tempted to say that the prosperity gospel is simply unchristian and foolish.[1] But I hesitate to do so. Apparently there are lot of people, a lot of Christians involved in this kind of teaching. They cannot be *all* unchristian and foolish, can they? If a majority of a population is wrong, most often it is the case because their beliefs are a perversion of genuine beliefs. Most superstitions are a perversion of genuine faith. If some parts of the prosperity gospel are superstitious, are unchristian and foolish, what is the genuine faith behind it, of which it is a perversion? What criteria do we have to determine where genuine faith ends and superstition begins? Finding these criteria might also help us to understand what the prosperity gospel is about: what it is saying, or trying to say. In this paper I want to look for such

---

1. By "unchristian" I simply mean factually not belonging to the Christian tradition, and by "foolish" something that is at odds with common sense. Note that I do not say that the prosperity gospel is unchristian and foolish, but only that I am *tempted* to describe it thus.

Part 3: THEOLOGICAL REFLECTION

criteria to distinguish between Christianity and superstition,[2] and between faith and foolishness, with regard to the prosperity gospel.

In order to find these criteria, let us begin with looking at what the prosperity gospel is.

What Is the Prosperity Gospel?

What the prosperity gospel is, becomes clearer when we look at the groups who are attracted to it, and why they are attracted to it. Therefore we will look at these questions first.

Who Is Attracted to the Prosperity Gospel?

The prosperity gospel is widespread in Africa. Paul Gifford, a researcher of African Christianity, connects the prosperity gospel with "middle-class religious entrepreneurs of the major cities" (1998:335). Anthropologist Birgit Meyer reaches similar conclusions in her survey of research on Christianity in Africa. She says: "These churches had tremendous appeal especially for young people, who seek to eschew gerontocratic hierarchies and aspire to progress in life (the upwardly mobile)" (2004:460). ("Gerontocratic" means "governed by old people.") The people who are attracted to the prosperity gospel are *not* the poorest of the poor, but especially the young, urban middle-class: the ones who either are moving upwards in society or aspire to do so, and the ones who would like to see changes in the way churches are organized, the hierarchy. These two characteristics are also related to why these people are attracted to the prosperity gospel.

Why Are These People Attracted to the Prosperity Gospel?[3]

The self-description of the preachers of the prosperity gospel is targeted at the way mainline churches speak about poverty. As Meyer says: "Many

---

2. In this article I speak as a systematic theologian. In the article "'Superstition' as a Contemplative Term: A Wittgensteinian Perspective" I have shown that even in a contemplative philosophy of religion it is possible to recognize this distinction between genuine faith and superstition (forthcoming).

3. Gifford and others see a relationship between the prosperity gospel on this continent and traditional African religion: "It is natural that the [Prosperity] Gospel should be so prevalent, because Africa's traditional religions were focused on material realities"

PCC's [Pentecostal churches] represent prosperity as a God-given blessing and resent the mainline churches for legitimizing poverty by referring to Jesus Christ as a poor man" (2004:459). Prosperity gospel preacher Duncan-Williams (quoted in Gifford 1998:79) says: "The traditional and orthodox churches we grew up in held many views which were diametrically opposed to God's word. [. . .] They preach a doctrine which says in essence: poverty promotes humility." By stressing how good and noble it is to be poor just like Jesus, the mainline churches would discredit everyone who prospers in life, or aspires to prosper in life. Whether or not this is a correct description of mainline theology, the prosperity gospel seems to attract people who, instead of feeling guilty about their progress in life, look for dignity in prosperity, or dignity in *aspiring* to prosperity.

The other aspect that attracts people to the prosperity gospel is the different way in which its churches tend to be organized. I heard someone describing the difference between Reformed and Pentecostal churches thus: "If you feel like singing a particular song, in the Pentecostal churches you just sing it, whereas in the Reformed churches you first have to ask permission from the elders." In the mainline churches, order, hierarchy, tradition and protocol are important, whereas the churches of the prosperity gospel present themselves as more free, less structured, more direct and personal. The prosperity gospel seems to attract people who, beyond tradition and protocol, look for dignity in their pure, spontaneous religious impulses.

What if We Say the Prosperity Gospel Is Foolish?

A mainline church theologian may think that sooner or later reality will catch up with the blatantly untrue message of the prosperity gospel. However, just waiting for the storm of the prosperity gospel to pass by may be interpreted as yet another sign of the condescending attitude of the elite, who the prosperity gospel is attacking. It may reinforce its critique.

Apart from that, we might wonder whether it makes sense to suggest that so many people are foolish. It looks like Birgit Meyer (2004: 460) sees the prosperity gospel as something foolish in this sense, when she says: "The Prosperity Gospel is at once PCC's [Pentecostal churches] main

---

(1998:335). I am hesitant in this respect since most often the parents and grandparents of the adherents to the prosperity gospel had already left Africa's traditional religions. Anyway, I will not focus here on this connection, but on the prosperity gospel as a protest movement within the Christian tradition.

attraction and, as the promise in the long run fails to materialise among most ordinary believers, its main weakness." But I would say the critique regarding the interpretation of rain dances by the important philosopher Ludwig Wittgenstein applies here. He criticized the idea that practices like rain dances and morning rituals are foolish, practiced by foolish people who think that their rituals cause the rain to fall or the sun to rise. If they really thought so, they would do rain dances in the dry season, instead of at the beginning of the rainy season. "Or again," as Wittgenstein says, "toward morning, when the sun is about to rise, rites of daybreak are celebrated by the people, but not during the night, when they simply burn lamps" (1993:137). Don't most adherents of the prosperity gospel simply go to work to earn their money, just like Abraham did before them? We need to look at the prosperity gospel not as a set of apparently false statements, but as a religious ritual, a puzzling ritual, that requires an examination of the way it is taken up in people's lives. How do they use it?

To regard the prosperity gospel as foolish is at once reinforcing its appeal and failing to do justice to what most of their adherents do in their day-to-day lives.

What if We Say the Prosperity Gospel Is Unchristian?

A mainline church theologian may want to point out what is theologically (or biblically or historically) wrong about the prosperity gospel: "They lack attention for finitude, for the cross; they contradict almost the entire theological tradition," etc. However true these critiques may be, at the same time they showcase your own intellectual skills and how important you think they are, while neglecting people who have to claim their dignity by something other than intellectual capacities.

Furthermore, showing that the claims of the prosperity gospel are biblically, theologically or historically incorrect does not explain why so many people are attracted to it. In this respect the prosperity gospel is parallel to the powerful discourse about autochthony and belonging, as the Dutch anthropologist Peter Geschiere recently traced it in Africa and Europe *The Perils of Belonging: Autochthony, Citizenship and Exclusion in Africa and Europe* (2009). ("Autochthony" means "born from the soil" and claims to it are often used to exclude outsiders.) Geschiere points out that the discourse of autochthony and belonging claims that true autochthones have more rights to the resources of a country than the cosmopolitan intellectual elite. If you are truly a Dutchman, or Ivorian, or whatever, then most of the resources available in that country are rightfully yours. And if you question the concept of a true Dutchman or Ivorian, that simply proves that you are not a Dutchman or Ivorian, you are probably a member of the cosmopolitan intellectual elite that momentarily claims the increasing resources of our globalizing world. A true Dutchman or Ivorian simply knows what it is to be truly Dutch or Ivorian.

Geschiere asks us to recognize on the one hand how blatantly untrue the claims of the discourse of autochthony and belonging are—the concepts of "simply Dutch" or "simply Ivorian" would not survive any historical scrutiny; however, on the other hand these claims have a strong emotional appeal. Geschiere points out that the discourse of autochthony and belonging uses a simple logic for non-intellectual, non-globalised people to gain access to the resources that globalization is making available mainly for intellectual, cosmopolitan people at the moment. This is the point where I suggest there is a striking similarity between the prosperity gospel and the discourse of autochthony and belonging. Geschiere who analyses this discourse in Europe and Africa says about the latter:

> Historicizing is only one step. Another challenge, and probably a more difficult one, is to understand that even if autochthony, again like other forms of belonging, is historically constructed—and can even be "debunked" as blatantly incorrect—it still takes on a "naturalness" that gives it its considerable emotional power and concomitant mobilizing force. (2009:169)

Both the discourse of belonging and the discourse of the prosperity gospel share a very strong emotional appeal despite, or, maybe *because of* their blatantly untrue, simple logic. This is connected to the anti-elitist thrust of these discourses. The prosperity gospel might represent a movement of dissent.

Geschiere notices that "the appeal to the local in autochthony discourse is often about defending special access to the national or the global" (2009:209). Precisely through stressing their *locality* locals indirectly reclaim their share of the *global* economy. I would say that in a similar way the apparently unspiritual appeal to material issues may often be about defending special access to the spiritual. The mainline churches in Africa seem to exclude those who prosper, and definitely those who want to prosper from the spiritual domain. In mainline churches it does not seem to be accepted to bluntly say: "I want to be rich." The aspiration to wealth is

Part 3: THEOLOGICAL REFLECTION

not suitable. Secondly, the mainline churches seem to exclude those who favor spontaneous religious impulses from the spiritual domain. Through stressing the importance of material wealth and defending that this view is biblically sound, a new generation might attempt to indirectly reclaim their access to the spiritual domain.

What Is the Prosperity Gospel?

The question that has puzzled me is: What can it mean to promise everyone health and wealth within a year, if they only believe or tithe? We have seen that instead of just focusing on these strange statements, we can also look at the prosperity gospel as a ritual, a puzzling ritual, that is taken up in people's lives. Instead of just debunking its statements as blatantly incorrect, we should pay attention to the strong emotional appeal that the prosperity gospel nonetheless has. The prosperity gospel need not be a foolish and unchristian way to attain health and wealth. The prosperity gospel might be a genuine protest against certain tendencies in the mainline churches, such as to discredit prospering, and to be formal, to exploit protocols to reduce spontaneity in church services. The prosperity gospel might be a celebration of the *dignity* in pure, spontaneous religious impulses and the *dignity* in enjoying or wishing to enjoy the good things in life.

Criteria for the Prosperity Gospel

The question remains of how we should judge the discourse that expresses this movement of reclaiming dignity. How can we distinguish between a genuine movement of dissent and a kind of dissent that simply is unchristian and foolish?

To find answers to these questions I want to compare the prosperity gospel's reading of Abraham, such as that of Otabil, the Ghanaian preacher quoted in the introduction, with Søren Kierkegaard's reading of Abraham as a knight of faith. Otabil claims that a believer cannot get poorer, if he has faith like Abraham had. In the story of Abraham, who had to sacrifice his son Isaac, Otabil sees a believer who obeys God, and God provides a ram. As a reward for his faith Abraham keeps his son, and both became rich. Kierkegaard's discourse about Abraham and the sacrifice of Isaac sounds very different, but there are also similarities that suggest Kierkegaard might help us to come up with criteria for a genuine prosperity gospel.

Kierkegaard's Abraham

In *Fear and Trembling*, Kierkegaard (as Johannes de Silentio) describes Abraham as the father of all believers. Going to Mount Moriah to sacrifice his son Isaac, Abraham showed what faith is. According to Kierkegaard (1843:139), faith consists in two movements:

> Abraham makes two movements. He makes the infinite movement of resignation and gives up his claim to Isaac, something no one can understand because it is a private undertaking. But then he further makes, and at every moment is making, the movement of faith. This is his comfort. For he says, "Nevertheless it won't happen, or if it does the Lord will give me a new Isaac on the strength of the absurd."

Abraham loves his son with all his heart. Nonetheless, he completely renounces his claims on him. He hands back to God what is rightfully God's. This movement of resignation is admirable and wonderful—to do this is what should be taught in churches. However Abraham makes one further movement, a movement that cannot be taught: the movement of faith. Abraham completely renounces his claims on Isaac; yet, simultaneously, he believes God will work it out so that he *has* Isaac.

This last movement can only be done in fear and trembling: until the end only God knows whether you are a murderer or a man of faith. In the task of resignation you can grow and become a little better every day; in the movement of faith it is all or nothing. Kierkegaard expresses this point in a provocative way when he says: "Abraham is . . . either a murderer or a man of faith. The middle-term that saves the tragic hero is something Abraham lacks" (1843:85). A "tragic hero" can be a little bit good, or on his way to the good; for Abraham as a man of faith, however, it is all or nothing. We can see that in his case it truly is "all" when we look at Abraham's ability to receive Isaac with joy after he had fully renounced him. Kierkegaard says: "What Abraham found the easiest of all would for me be hard, to find joy again in Isaac!" (1843:65). If you have renounced him with all your heart, how can you love him again without double-mindedness, without doubts that you did not renounce him with all your heart and therefore are just fooling yourself to think that you have faith? First, in the movement of resignation Abraham gave up his son Isaac completely, but secondly, in the movement of faith, he receives him again in great joy, without any sign of resignation.

Part 3: THEOLOGICAL REFLECTION

Kierkegaard's approach resembles the approach of the prosperity gospel in two respects. Firstly, both stress that faith is, in the end, something beyond what can be taught and regulated: Abraham in his movement of faith cannot be judged by church protocol, but only by God. Secondly, both stress that to have faith is not at odds with enjoying the good things in life; Abraham, in fact, did show his faith by enjoying his offspring after renouncing him and receiving him back.

If we do not want to dismiss the prosperity gospel completely, then, looking at the comparison of the prosperity gospel and Kierkegaard's Abraham, how can we distinguish genuine from superstitious forms of the prosperity gospel? Kierkegaard says that a knight of faith in the end can only be judged by God, but that, nonetheless, even from outside this individual relationship we can determine some criteria: "Whether the individual is now really in a state of temptation or a knight of faith, only the individual can decide. Still, it is possible on the basis of the paradox to construct certain criteria which even someone not in it can understand" (1843:106). Therefore, to conclude this paper I will present four tentative criteria.

Gratitude instead of Manipulation

First of all, Abraham did not manipulate God into giving his blessing. He also received Isaac back in gratitude. He rejoiced in his good fortune "on the strength of the absurd, for all human calculation had long since been suspended" (Kierkegaard 1843:65). Abraham did not make the movements of resignation and faith because he knew that they were the right tricks to get what he wanted. There was no guarantee that things would turn out right; in fact, everything pointed in the opposite direction. Abraham acted in complete conflict with worldly sagacity, and manipulation played no part in it at all. The prosperity gospel should, similarly, be an expression of gratitude, not a manipulation of a rather mechanical God.

Just like people who celebrate rites of the coming of day, and at the same time simply burn lamps at night, the prosperity gospel should not be something to replace ordinary means to find health and wealth. The prosperity gospel should be a way to express gratitude for what God gives in ordinary ways.

Recognizing the Value of Tradition and Resignation

Kierkegaard says that whoever thinks it is simple enough to be like Abraham and enjoy the gift of faith, can be sure that he does not have faith (1843:103). Faith is not simple, and a knight of faith like Abraham knows that it is glorious to be part of a faith tradition, and glorious to seek to renounce, more and more, our attachments to worldly goods (cf. 1843:103). Although he follows another path himself, he recognizes this. Abraham recognizes that it is wonderful to be able to see nobility in poverty. Abraham himself was only able to make the movement of faith—receiving Isaac back once again—*after* he had made the movement of resignation with all his heart.

The prosperity gospel should not deem it easy to have faith while enjoying the good things in life; neither should it despise those who try to renounce their claims on earthly goods. If you do either of those things, you surely are not a knight of faith like Abraham.

Acting Personally and in Fear and Trembling

The first explicit criterion that Kierkegaard mentions is,

> The true knight of faith is always in absolute isolation.... The sectarians [however] deafen each other with their clang and clatter, [and think they are] storming heaven.... As for the knight of faith, he is assigned to himself alone, he has the pain of being unable to make himself intelligible to others but feels no vain desire to show others the way.... The true knight of faith is a witness, never a teacher. (1843:106f)

Whether you are really enjoying the good things in life as an act of faith, rather than of worldliness, is not something that can be judged from the outside. Only God knows this and you, like Abraham, in fear and trembling, can only hope that you judge yourself correctly. You cannot prove it, you cannot boast on it, you cannot teach it to others, since from the outside there is no difference between someone who is insane and a believer, no difference between a murderer and a man of faith—so claims Kierkegaard, since Abraham was willing to kill his own son (1843:85, 103). Only in fear and trembling did Abraham know that he was no murderer when he climbed Mount Moriah.

Part 3: THEOLOGICAL REFLECTION

Similarly, a genuine kind of prosperity gospel would be a lonely thing. It would be something for the individual, to enjoy only in fear and trembling.

It Is About God, and not About You

Kierkegaard says: "He who loves God without faith reflects on himself, while the person who loves God reflects on God" (1843:66). Kierkegaard does *not* mean that it is wrong to reflect on yourself. Someone who has not reached the faith of Abraham, but who is on his way to renouncing his claims on worldly goods, *needs* to reflect on himself. However, if someone, like Abraham, is enjoying his blessings as an act of faith, he must be reflecting on God rather than on himself. Isaac, but also Abraham's faith itself, was a gift from God and not something that reflected Abraham himself and his achievements. The focus should always be on God and his works. This is the fourth and final criterion I want to propose here to judge whether a prosperity gospel is genuine.

Conclusion

There is dignity in pure, spontaneous religious impulses, and there is dignity in enjoying or wishing to enjoy the good things in life. However, we have to be very careful. Looking at these four proposed criteria might help to distinguish what is valuable and what is not, in tendencies towards prosperity gospel in our churches.

Bibliography

Geschiere, P. 2009. *The Perils of Belonging: Autochthony, Citizenship, and Exclusion in Africa and Europe*. Chicago: University of Chicago Press.
Gifford, P. 1998. *African Christianity: Its Public Role*. Bloomington: Indiana University Press.
Kierkegaard, S. 1843. *Fear and Trembling*. Translated by A. Hannay. Repr., 1985. London: Penguin Classics.
Kroesbergen, H. T. Forthcoming. "'Superstition' as a Contemplative Term: A Wittgensteinian Perspective."
Meyer, B. 2004. "Christianity in Africa: From African Independent to Pentecostal-Charismatic Churches." *Annual Review of Anthropology* 33:447–74.
Wittgenstein, L. 1993. *Philosophical Occasions: 1912-1951*. Edited by J. Klagge and A. Nordmann. Indianapolis: Hackett Publishing Company.

PART 4

Cultural Analysis

7

"Zambia Dziko la Chonde"[1]

LUKAS SOKO

THIS ARTICLE PROVIDES A practical-theological descriptive assessment of the factors relevant to the understanding of one of the new waves of preaching in Africa, called the prosperity gospel. In many of our mainline churches, particularly in urban congregations, the practice of prosperity preaching is becoming one of the salient contemporary issues—not only in Zambia but in Africa at large. The researcher believes that a better understanding of the factors influencing mainline churches on the prosperity gospel can help the leadership of the church to orient their members to take a balanced position. The motivation to undertake this research emerges from the current trend in which the prosperity gospel, with its promises of material-spiritual blessings, challenges the Reformed tradition: our "Reformed theology and ecclesiology."

To aid the reader's understanding, I will first give a brief background of factors that influenced Zambia from 1990 to date. This phase is crucial in understanding the current trends of Christianity in Zambia. Secondly, I will describe some important contextual factors that have changed Zambian society, and Africa in general, in many ways. The basic assumption

---

1. "Zambia dziko la chonde": In vernacular the expression implies a country which has vast fertility land. "Chonde" simply means land whose fertility can allow almost every crop to be grown even without using advanced technology. In this article, "Zambia dziko la chonde" signifies the many opportunities the mushrooming religions have found in Zambia even when their background is questionable.

is that the social influences of globalization, economy and politics have a direct influence on society. For the church, being both sacred and social, it is impossible to escape these influences. Thirdly, the article will discuss the impact of electronic churches on our "Reformed worship."

The Dawn of Multiparty Democracy in Zambia: 1990 to Date

Zambia has passed through different phases in her political history (Soko 2010:20–39): the colonial phase (1880s to 1964); the independence phase (1964–1990); and the multiparty democracy phase (1990–date). This dawn of multiparty democracy is important in understanding the factors that are influencing Zambian society in different ways. During the independence phase two things happened: 1. Zambia was declared a one-party state on 13 December 1972 (Erdman and Simutanyi 2003:3–4; Ranker 2005:52) 2. In 1988 President Kenneth Kaunda imposed a ban on the registration of new churches (Wikipedia 2012).

However, on 17 December 1990, then-President Kenneth Kaunda repealed the constitution to allow registration of many parties (Mwanzah 2011). And on 31 October 1991 the first ever multiparty general elections were held to elect a new government. The Movement for Multiparty Democracy (MMD) won the election with a landslide victory. The MMD under Fredrick Chiluba became the ruling government, partially through the strong support of the Christian fraternity (Soko 2010:38).

The events that followed immediately with the new government have continued to influence the Zambian people. Of importance is the declaration of Zambia as a "Christian nation."[2] This declaration implicitly meant that the ban on the registration of new churches was lifted. Under this declaration many new waves of worship started mushrooming. To implement this declaration in Zambian society the Religious Desk was established at the State House. It is during this period that Zambia witnessed the rise of Pentecostalism and televangelists. This phenomenon has challenged the landscape of the Christian faith in Zambia to this day.

The changes during the Chiluba period show that, even as different traditional practices and ecclesiologies were sought to define and protect the church from external influences, social forces intruded through this dynamic and reshaped mainline churches' traditions. In light of the prosperity gospel, which poses a threat to Reformed worship in Africa, and

2. For the detailed discussion read Soko 2010:38–40.

which has already taken root, the mainline churches are called to engage in a dialectical hermeneutic with their context. By "dialectical hermeneutic" the researcher refers to the dialogical process in which the Church must endeavor to explore a critical debate between the faith tradition of the past and the new realities that confront the Church (Soko 2010:47).

In order to reach a better understanding of global tendencies and their influence on Zambian society and specifically the Church, the researcher will briefly discuss the concept of globalization.

Globalization and its Influence on Christianity

Soko (2010:49-50) says globalization can be interpreted as an interconnectedness of the general macro affairs of countries and communities, and the interactions and processes of human integration through networks that alter the lifestyle of individuals. He further says globalization involves a change of values and choices, as well as a deconstruction and reconstruction of identities. In religion, the influence of globalization transcends traditional values. The major influence of globalization in the churches is the constant movement it brings about. Globalization is an unpredictable, ever-changing force that does not stop at the boundaries of any given church.

The term globalization designates "a socially constructed economic process that has assumed the status of an economic necessity and an ideological imperative" (Rumscheidt 1998:4). Rumscheidt cites the shift in investment, production, and trade decisions from serving national markets to serving world markets; the decline in trade barriers; and the shrinking of communications, transportation time, and cost as examples of processes which are now present in almost every part of the world.

Castells (2006:72) defines globalization in terms of social movements. He argues that "globalization is enhanced by informationalization enacted by networks of wealth, technology and power." Giddens (1991:32;35;55) defines globalization in terms of the dialectical interplay of the local and the global, where individuals are forced to negotiate lifestyle choices among a diversity of options.

The above-mentioned perspectives on globalization reveal that it has economic, political, cultural, and technological aspects that may be closely intertwined. In most cases, these aspects of globalization are key influences on individuals' quality of life. The social benefits and the costs that globalization brings upon them generate strong debate about the orientation of both individuals and churches. In this article, the focus is on the economic aspects of globalization.

Economic Aspects

The economic consequence of globalization is perceived to be the increased integration of nations becoming more interdependent, with greater investment opportunities. Gosh and Guven (2006:70–71) say that a perception exists that trans-border trade and investment offer tremendous and often unprecedented economic opportunities as a vehicle of economic progress and prosperity for nations. According to Maloka and Le Roux (2001:65) the rationale is: developing countries that act individually cannot survive the vicious forces of globalization.

In line with the above perspectives, economic globalization has resulted in a gradual shift in our churches. In Africa, one of the key aspects of globalization is its influence on the church through electronic churches and their preaching. Electronic churches are churches that address their members or adherents through the radio, television, internet and open crusade revivals. As economic aspects of globalization lean more on trans-border trade worldwide, this also brings about changes in the cultural orientation of each individual country. Restrictions on goods and services are sidelined, more choices are allowed, and thus a devolution of power takes place that leaves traditional practices in a less favored position in society. As a result, each community or country continues to be exposed to a wide range of choices in cultural orientation and values, and the potential for adaptation constantly confronts our worldviews.

Mooney and Evans (2007:39) state that the key component in the global spread of consumerism has been the growth of mass media and advertising with the rise of global brands. They argue, "Through advertising, consumers are urged to align themselves with the identities, values and lifestyles that a given commodity expresses."

As a result of this influence it appears everyone is adopting consumerist behavior in individual dress, software, music, and worship. Even our staple food basket nowadays comes from across the world. Thus, individuals are able to access these items without much restriction. The question still remains of what are the contextual factors that influence the prosperity gospel in Zambia? Three levels of contextual factors—macro, meso and micro—will be analyzed in order to determine whether any of these factors correlates with prosperity gospel.

The Macro-aspects of Globalization that Influence Zambian Society

According to the World Bank (2007:33), macro-level analysis is about understanding the country and its context. The macro-level analysis aims to contribute toward an understanding of the significance of the historical context: the political ideological climate, political institutional culture, and economic and social makeup of countries. The current influence of electronic churches on mainline churches, resulting in differences in the mode of worship, cannot be explained without understanding the influence of global Christianity on Zambia and Africa at large.

Hendriks (2004:77) says the electronic age of information brings other cultures, influences and world events to local congregations almost daily. Miles and Scott (2002:3) say that the overall or aggregate implications of tens of thousands of individual decisions that companies and households make generate the macro-level aspects' outcomes.

Arising from these macro-aspects of globalization, it can be noted that, today, the growth of Pentecostal, Independent and electronic churches has become a global phenomenon. These movements (Pentecostal, Independent and electronic churches) were originally perceived as sects, and today have become worldwide churches/denominations that have to some extent led to the decline of mainline churches. Today such movements, often called the "global Christianity" movement, are perceived to have mushroomed in Zambia during the post-independence period.

Electronic Churches: The Case for Zambia

In Zambia, Christianity has strong overtones of Pentecostalism,[3] which has become an increasingly prominent feature of Zambia's religious and

3. According to Barret and Johnson (2001:860), "Pentecostalism/-ist" is a general descriptive noun or adjective for any person, group or movement that stresses the Holy Spirit's direct divine inspiration, which is presented in glossalia, faith healing and parallel phenomena. In Zambia, individuals associated themselves with such tendencies that were/are perceived to be Pentecostal. At the beginning of the early 1990s in Zambia's new political dispensation, this trend became a force to be reckoned with. The Pentecostal movements in Zambia share the view that mainline Churches of the missionary era have a rigid Christian spirituality. Based on their understanding, mainline Churches

political landscape. Statistics are very complicated to calculate and verify, but some estimates for Christian affiliations since the country's dawn of democratization reveal amazing trends in the way these so-called Pentecostal churches have taken root in Zambia.

According to Jenkins (2007:1) and Walls (2002:85), global Christianity is one of the transforming movements in the history of religion worldwide. Both note that, over the last century, the centre of gravity in Christianity worldwide has shifted southwards, to Africa and Latin America without any possibility of stopping its impact. This movement challenges especially the mainline church leadership to distinguish between Christianity's different forms, and to comprehend the continued diversities in their mission orientations. The mainline churches must learn to resist a narrow church tradition and further apply their energies to the social and environmental challenges that face our globe.

Based on the developments of global Christianity, electronic churches have openly challenged the long-inherited missionary traditions. These have become no longer acceptable in the lives of members who have been exposed to many other worshiping practices. In our present context in Zambia three main factors are worth mentioning that have influenced the prosperity gospel. As has been already alluded to, these are: the arrival of multiparty democracy, the declaration of Zambia a Christian nation, and the media. This article does not intend to discuss all these aspects in detail, but will only highlight some influences of the media which the electronic churches have taken advantage of.

The Golden Age of Electronic Churches

Our understanding of the modern practice of faith (Christianity) is challenged as never before to start embracing the global "Christian culture." This new, globalised Christian culture seems to establish guidelines and social values that the church at large has begun to accept for her members. The collapse of the era of Christendom, coupled with the modern trend of globalization, leaves the church caught, even in worship, between its faithful adherence to tradition on one hand and human freedom on the other. The prosperity gospel creates a tension in many of the mainline

---

are witnessing a series of conflicts and schisms that, for example, took place in the RCZ because of their rigid adherence to tradition and their disobedience in not listening to the Holy Spirit.

denominations on the relationship between our ecclesiologies and popular prosperity gospel preaching.

Today the media has become liberalized, which is visible in the global distribution of media images that appear in the newspapers, television, radio and computer screens (Soko 2010:64). Sklair (2002:42) says that we now have a homogenizing mass media-based culture that, in turn, threatens national and local cultures and identities drives global culture in globalization. Today in Zambia, electronic churches have more air space on Zambian national television than any mainline denomination. Guder (1998:234–35) notes that electronic churches allow a large number of people to have a religious worship service without having a formal face-to-face relationship with members of a particular community. In a way both the clergy and the laity can attend extra church services in their homes and still claim their allegiance to their old denomination.

Arising from this phenomenon, the prosperity gospel cannot only be attributed to poverty situations but possibly to what I would call "worship plagiarism."[4] The issue of poverty is a reality. It impacts our lives and society on a daily basis. It is true that the church needs sound financial capital but how this is related to members leaves much to be desired. Globalization has no authority of censorship; just influence. Through globalization, the religious and the church polity dimensions continue to face challenges in their endeavor to examine what doctrines and practices to accept and reject.

Our Faith Response to Emerging Needs

Most of our members in the mainline churches feel that missionary Christianity does not adequately meet their emerging needs in society. Kalu (2005:281) and Paas (2006:142) point to the problem of, and deliverance from, evil. The missionaries tended to view evil philosophically, whereas the Africans regard evil functionally. Secondly, the Christian orientation from this missionary perspective did not in concrete terms balance the obedience to the law of God and the reward in a material way. For, today, those who are faithful in the Lord and under the will of God expect material blessings. Since electronic churches use the radio, television, internet and open crusade revivals, their influence is great in our society. Whilst we can claim to be poor in our definition of poverty, ironically everyone has

---

4. Worship plagiarism is here in this article described as a syndrome of copying another faith practice without adequate knowledge about the practice.

access to the media. In urban areas nearly every Christian has a radio, a television set, a cell phone, and likely even internet access, all of which are direct tools that electronic churches use to reach out to their audiences. On both public and private television and radio stations one can hear 24-hour broadcasting services.

These factors, and certainly others as well, provide the backdrop to the emerging prosperity gospel across Africa. These factors have affected particularly those who are experiencing a transitional phase from bondage to the missionary church structures, to the current electronic church influence.

This influence of the prosperity gospel is critical to the mainline churches, because global Christianity has shown that, wherever the Church exists, its members are both gathered in corporate life and dispersed in society for the sake of God's mission in the world. With its many cultural and ethnic members who contribute their gifts, the pattern of modern trends in Christianity challenges the mainline churches to reconsider their dominant faith practices.

The vibrancy, sense of belonging, moral socialization, and community stability of mainline churches in Zambia are at stake, because of these developments—the simple adherence to inherited religious traditions is no longer sufficient in addressing the people's faith expectations. The advent of global Christianity in Zambia and Africa has given rise to a paradigm shift in leadership and worship, particularly in the mainline churches.

Conclusion

In summary, this article has examined the democratic phase of Zambia's history and the macro changes that have affected Zambian society. As also stated earlier in this article, the effects of globalization and the rise of Pentecostalism are closely connected. When the world became a "global village," a networked society emerged. The global cultural onslaughts have underlined the question: How can specific identities survive in the face of diversity?

Through the influence of the mass media, especially television and now the internet, everyone in the world can be exposed to the same images almost instantly, such as movies, television, music, worship and videos (Sklair 2002:43; Romanowski 2007:15). The capacity of globalization to fire the imagination has resulted in a lot of controversy in the mainline churches, which are concerned with loss of values, meaning and a worldview. The changes brought about by globalization have planted seeds that eventually sprout into new patterns of worship, even in many mainline churches. "Zambia dziko la chonde," as the title is of this article, Zambia the fertile land. Zambia has proven to be fertile land for many new mushrooming churches indeed.

Against this background, globalization and the rise of electronic churches in Zambia challenge the mainline churches in several ways to rethink even their public role and witness in society.

We cannot continue to demonize the current trends of globalization and the prosperity gospel too vehemently. What we must come to terms with is the fact that the flow of information moves quickly through the media, television, radio, CDs, video, music, satellite, et cetera. The flow of people from one country to another is also greater today than ever before in history.

The new realities of globalization and electronic churches require mainline church leadership to be flexible and capable of adjusting to diversity. Church leadership must be sufficiently flexible in order to respond meaningfully and in time to current needs, challenges and opportunities. Discernment is needed, rather than always being reactive.

Bibliography

Barrett, D. B., and T. M. Johnson. 2001. *World Christian Encyclopedia: A Comparative Survey of Churches and Religion in the Modern World.* 2nd ed. New York: Oxford University Press.
Castells, M. 2004. *The Power of Identity.* Oxford: Blackwell Publishing.
Erdmann, G., and N. Simuntanyi. 2003. *Transition in Zambia: The Hybridization of the Third Republic.* Lilongwe: Konrad-Adenauer-Stiftung.
Ghosh, B. N., and H. M. Guven. 2006. *Globalization and the Third World: A Study of NegativeConsequences.* New York: Palgrave Macmillan.
Giddens, A. 1991. *Modernity and Self-Identity: Self and Society in the Late Modern Age.* Cambridge: Polity Press.
Guder, D. L. 1998. *Missional Church: A Vision for the Sending of the Church in North America.* Grand Rapids, MI: Eerdmans.
Hendriks, H. J. 2004. *Studying Congregations in Africa.* Wellington: Lux Verbi BM.
Jenkins, P. 2002. *The Next Christendom: The Coming of Global Christianity.* New York: Oxford University Press.
Kalu, O., ed. 2005. *African Christianity: An African Story.* Sunnyside: Business Print Centre.
Maloka, E., and E. Le Roux. 2001. *Africa in the New Millennium.* Pretoria: Africa Institute of South Africa.

Part 4: CULTURAL ANALYSIS

Miles, D., and A. Scott. 2002. *Macroeconomics: Understanding the Wealth of Nations.* Chichester: Wiley.

Mooney, A., and B. Evans. 2007. *Globalization: The Key Concepts.* Abingdon: Routledge.

Mwanzah, T. 2011. "Remiscences of Chiluba." [online]. Available at: http://www.scribd.com/doc/100125597/Reminiscences-of-Chiluba.

Paas, S. 2006. *The Faith Moves South: A History of the Church in Africa.* Limbe: Assemblies of God Press.

Romanowski, W. D. 2007. *Eyes Wide Open: Looking for God in Popular Culture.* Grand Rapids, MI: Brazos Press.

Rumschiedt, B. 1998. *No Room for Grace: Pastoral Theology and Dehumanization in the Global Economy.* Grand Rapids, MI: Eerdmans.

Sklair, L. 2002. *Globalization, Capitalism and Its Alternatives.* New York: Oxford University Press.

Soko, L. 2010. *A Practical Theological Assessment of the Schism in the Reformed Church in Zambia (1996–2001).*Stellenbosch: Stellenbosch University.

Walls, A. F. 2002. *The Cross-Cultural Process in Christian History.* Oxford: Blackwell Publishing.

Wikipedia. 2012. "History of Christianity in Zambia." Wikipedia [online]. Available at: http://en.wikipedia.org/wiki/History_of_Christianity_in_Zambia.

World Bank. 2007. *Tools for Institutional, Political, and Social Analysis of Policy Reform: A Sourcebook for Development Practitioners.* Washington, DC: World Bank.

8

Dreams and Nightmares of Modernity
Accusations and Testimonies of Satanism in Zambia

JOHANNEKE KROESBERGEN-KAMPS

AREN'T WE ALL LOOKING for a comfortable life, unburdened by worries about illness and need? For students at Justo Mwale Theological University College, modernity and the process of becoming "modern" are intrinsically linked to acquiring more wealth and better health. But whereas in classical sociological theory modernity is thought to go hand in hand with secularization and a decline in the social relevance of religion, in Zambia Christianity and modernity seem to be a package deal.

Christianity, modernity and globalization are important forces in Zambia's urban areas. These forces are expected to bring development and prosperity. But have they really brought the measure of health and wealth that people have been looking for? For some the answer would be yes—but many more are experiencing poverty and need in the face of unattainable riches. The happy few that have prospered are commonly mistrusted. Questions are raised: Did he acquire his wealth in a legitimate way, or were other, darker, powers involved? Dreams of modernity can all too easily turn into a nightmare of alleged Satanic rituals.

Part 4: CULTURAL ANALYSIS

Is it a coincidence that especially in Pentecostal churches, with their emphasis on prosperity, testimonies of involvement in Satanism are quite popular? In this article I want to place Zambian accusations and testimonies of Satanism in the context of the search for modernity, health and wealth.

The Promised Land of Modernity

The eminent sociologist Anthony Giddens describes modernity as follows:

> A shorthand term for modern society, or industrial civilization. Portrayed in more detail, it is associated with (1) a certain set of attitudes towards the world, the idea of the world as open to transformation, by human intervention; (2) a complex of economic institutions, especially industrial production and a market economy; (3) a certain range of political institutions, including the nation-state and mass democracy. (Giddens and Pierson 1998:94)

In this description, Giddens positions modernity as an objective, value-free concept. The history of the concept of modernity, though, is more complex. In nineteenth century anthropological and sociological thought, there is a widespread belief in a progressive development of culture. Encouraged by scientific discoveries, which led to both industrialization and improvements in medical care, thus increasing human control over the environment (cf. Stolz 1997:195), evolutionist social thinkers thought that societies were destined to become modern and in that way would gain health and wealth for everyone.

The students with whom I discussed the definition of modernity were inclined to agree with this older teleological view of modernity, rather than with Giddens' use of modernity as a descriptive concept. "We have schools now, and don't hold our traditional beliefs anymore. That is civilization, isn't it? Everyone should be able to go to school or to a hospital whenever he needs it!" Education, health care, infrastructure: these are the aspects of modernity that have brought civilization to Zambia. Evolutionist theories may have lost their attraction in anthropology and sociology, but they have long influenced (and may still influence) Western dealings with Africa (cf. Ellis 2011) and, consequently, the way in which Africans perceive modernity. My students seem to take the stance that Ferguson describes in his book on the expectations of modernity in Zambia: "according [to the grand narrative of progress] the native population was moving rapidly along an avenue leading to 'civilization,' later styled 'Westernization' or 'modernization'" (1999:34).

So the idea that modernity will bring health and wealth is not unique to my students. In an article on the trade in second-hand clothing in Zambia, Tranberg Hansen notes the same construction of the modern as education, occupation and wealth. "Unlike anthropologists who have been taught to be wary of the predictions of modernization theory, few Zambians have qualms about the promises of modernization," she writes (1999:207). In the Zambian situation the concept of modernity has become part of a larger discourse of expectations for the attainable future. Ferguson discovers the same tendency in his conversations with mineworkers in the Copperbelt area:

> Modernization theory had become a local tongue, and sociological terminology and folk classifications had become disconcertingly intermingled in informants' intimate personal narratives. . . . [T]hat which once presented itself as *explicans* was beginning to make itself visible as *explicandum*. (1999:84, italics in original).

In this local discourse, modernity is almost portrayed as a promised land, a place somewhere down the road, where health and wealth will be abundant.

This *emic* use of the concept of modernity has little to do with Giddens's definition. Distinctions that are implicit in the scholarly use of modernity work differently in this local discourse. A striking example is the relationship between modernity and religion. According to Weber, the process of modernity is closely related to rationalization, secularization and disenchantment (cf. Dobbelaere 2009). Although the theory of secularization is heavily debated (pro: cf. Bruce 2002; contra: cf. Stark 1999), most sociologists agree that (religious) traditions have lost authority in modern societies (cf. Giddens 1998; Thompson 1996; Heelas and Woodhead 2005). In the interpretative scheme behind much sociological and anthropological thought, "religion" and "tradition" are opposed to "the secular," "rational thinking" and "modernity."[1]

The local, Zambian, discourse of modernity uses a different distinction. "Rational thinking" and "modernity" are still together at one side,

---

1. Literature on religion and modernity, in Africa and elsewhere, tries to show how modernity and religion co-exist or how they depend on each other (see for example: Comaroff and Comaroff 1993; Fardon, van Binsbergen and van Dijk 1999; Geschiere 1997; Meyer and Pels 2003; Moore and Sanders 2001), but still the distinction between "the religious" and "the secular" is an (often implicit) underlying assumption.

opposed to "tradition" and "the village"—so far no different from the conceptual scheme in social and anthropological thought. The big difference, though, is the place of Christianity in this scheme. Social scientists would see Christianity as one example of "the religious." In discussions with students it has become clear to me that they place Christianity next to "rational thinking" and "modernity." Christianity came to Zambia with the promise of development. Christianity, commerce and civilization go together, was Livingstone's mindset. This made Christianity from the beginning an interesting option for those who wanted to leave "tradition" behind and become educated, rich and influential (cf. Meyer 1999). In this local discourse, the promised land of modernity is, foremost, a Christian country.

The Ambiguities of Modernity

For many Zambians, the dreams of modernity have not materialized. Although the current economic situation in Zambia is better than during the depression of the 1980s and 1990s that Ferguson describes (1999), according to the World Bank in 2006 59 percent of the population lived below the poverty line. Life expectancy in Zambia was forty-eight years in 2009 and an estimate of one in seven Zambians aged between fifteen and forty-nine is HIV positive (World Databank 2012). Zambia may be a Christian nation according to its constitution; yet it is no promised land of health and wealth. This may induce a sense of disappointment in mission churches: they have not been able to bring prosperity and have given little protection against illness.

Worse, it seems that modernity, far from being all good, brings its own problems as well. In a liberal economy, inequalities seem to grow rather than lessen; there is talk of exploitation of Zambian resources by multinational companies from all over the world. Families and communities break up in the wake of the quest for a more comfortable life (cf. Udelhoven 2009b). John and Jean Comaroff describe this world:

> [It is] a world in which ends far outstrip means, in which the will to consume is not matched by the opportunity to earn, in which there is a high velocity of exchange and a relatively low volume of production. And yet, we repeat, it is a world in which the *possibility of* rapid enrichment, of amassing a fortune by largely invisible methods, is always palpably present. (1999:293, italics in original)

Billboards and shopping malls show the urban citizens what money can buy. Some have even become rich; but for the majority modernity has not brought the dreamed-for prosperity.

In this climate, those happy few that have attained wealth or political power are under close scrutiny: How did they do it? Was there *juju* involved?[2] Rumors of occult powers, invoked to accumulate wealth, are widespread. In his classical study on witchcraft among the Azande, Evans-Pritchard stated: "Those whom we would call good citizens—and, of course, the richer and more powerful members of society are such—are seldom accused of witchcraft" (2010 [1937]:249). Today it seems that precisely the richer and more powerful members of society are a target for accusations of witchcraft or Satanism (cf. Geschiere 1997; Comaroff and Comaroff 1999). People long for prosperity, but in the current climate of suspicion, and of prosperity for only a few, it is believed that those who have achieved it must have used illegitimate means (cf. Moore 1999:306). In a recent case, three citizens, one of them a relatively successful businessman, were burned to death by an angry mob in a Chambishi compound. In the online comments to the newspaper article on *Zambian Watchdog*, not even the president is beyond suspicion: "Thez fools, isn't this w@ they voted 4? W@ do u xpect wen de Head of State is a satanist? [sic]."

Religious communities can fall under the suspicion of Satanism as easily as individuals can. When, in 2005, the Universal Church of the Kingdom of God was building a large, new church in the centre of Lusaka, the building site was destroyed by a mob that suspected Satanism. This (Pentecostal) church, which earlier sparked controversy in its homeland Brazil and in South Africa, allegedly gives members charmed credit cards that register no debt (Comaroff and Comaroff 1999:291). In Zambia, reports of human sacrifice led to a ban on this church, which was lifted after one month. Ironically, the Universal Church of the Kingdom of God highly emphasizes spiritual warfare against the powers of evil and practices exorcisms regularly.

Accusations of involvement in occult practices are reinforced by testimonies of former witches and ex-Satanists. For my students these testimonies are evidence for the existence of witchcraft and Satanism. And a churchgoer said: "I didn't know there were that many Satanists, but now I've

---

2. The term *juju* originates in West Africa, where it referred to ancestral spirits. Over time it became a catchphrase for any sort of African occult practices, which is widely used in Zambian media—if not in scholarly literature.

seen a confession in my own church. They are everywhere." Popular fears of Satanism become even more real when they are enacted in a testimony in a church service (Frankfurter 2006:181, cf. Behrend 2007). In December 2011, a member of parliament confessed in front of his congregation to have practiced Satanism before being born again. A confession like this is not unique in Zambia, although in most cases the ex-Satanists are young adults, and often female (Udelhoven 2009a).

In Zambia, dreams of modernity have not come true for the majority. Prosperity has even become a source of suspicion. These suspicions are further reinforced by public confessions of occult practices.

Exploring Testimonies of Satanism

The description "occult practices" can refer to many different things. In this article I focus on Satanism; but what is the difference—if there is any—between Satanism and witchcraft? Satanism has become a popular description for a variety of occult practices in Zambia since the 1990s (Udelhoven 2008). The concept of Satanism in Zambia is clearly connected to older discourses on witchcraft and possession, but there are differences as well. A Zambian ex-Satanist described the difference as follows: "Witches and Satanists are of the same school. But while witches have the power only of grade 1 or 2 . . . , Satanists are advanced: they have reached grade 11 or 12" (Udelhoven 2008:1). Comaroff and Comaroff note a similar statement: satanism is high-octane witchcraft" (1999:292). Whereas witchcraft is linked to "the village" (cf. Ashfort 1996:1210), Satanism is thought to be an urban, international and global phenomenon. Witchcraft is connected to "traditional beliefs," whereas Satanism makes sense in the context of a dualistic Christianity.

In this article I will use the confession "Ex-Satanist Gideon Mulenga—Set Free by Jesus!" (Testimonies of Heaven and Hell 2011) as a case study, because it is the most lengthy and detailed first-hand confession from Zambia that I could find. When necessary I will discuss this confession in relationship to other testimonies from Zambia and other African countries. In Zambia Father Bernard Udelhoven of the (Roman Catholic) Faith and Encounter Centre Zambia (FENZA) has published several interesting articles on the subject of Satanism (2008; 2009a; 2009b; 2009c; 2010). Birgit Meyer (1999), Jean and John Comaroff (1999), Misty Bastian (2001) and

David Frankfurter (2006) have also written lengthily on confessions of ex-Satanists in Africa.

One question that has to be addressed before we look more closely at Mr. Mulenga's testimony is: Did it really happen? Does this Satanic organization really exist? The accusations of occult practices are very real; people are being killed and properties are destroyed because of them. On the other hand, although the U.S.-based "Church of Satan" is referred to in confessions of Satanists, there is no evidence that this religious movement is actually active in Zambia. So what is this Satanism that is talked about in the confessions? To interpret testimonies of involvement with Satanism as "merely symbolic" is not to take seriously the beliefs and experiences of accusers and confessors alike. The experiences that the testimonies talk about have been very real for the ex-Satanists and for the congregations that hear them. Even so, I think that a testimony like this is more than a description of facts that happened; it is the expression of a (Christian) worldview with its own values and expectations (cf. Oldridge 2012:48; Frankfurter 2006:204). From the transcript of the interview it is clear that Mr. Mulenga is not always telling factual truths. When talking of Satanism, he sometimes refers to an organization of evil, in which you need to be initiated. At other times he interprets Satanism as humans being sinful:

> Satanism is when a person is like Satan. A person is like Satan when he begins to do things that Satan does: telling lies, gossiping, killing people, adultery: a lot of sins that are happening. All those sins ... when a person is doing that, he is representing Satan.

This is a shift from Satanism as an organization to which you can belong, to Satanism as a state of mind. I think other parts of the interview are also more, or something other, than factual descriptions of what happened.

Acting out Dreams and Nightmares of Modernity

Gideon Mulenga shares his story of Satanism with a Norwegian Reverend, Jan-Aage Torp. A video capture of the testimony has been circulating on the internet since 2007. The video is shared on many websites, in a number of cases only recently posted—clearly his story is still quite popular. Mr. Mulenga is also actively sharing his confession in popular overnight prayer sessions and deliverance services. On the video we see Mr. Mulenga, smartly dressed in a suit, sitting on a couch in what seems to be a living

Part 4: CULTURAL ANALYSIS

room. He is interviewed by Rev. Torp (wearing a shirt in the colors of the Zambian flag), who sits on a chair opposite Mr. Mulenga.

According to the interview, Mr. Mulenga was initiated into Satanism by his mother at a tender age. He was ordered to sacrifice many people, some of them family members. Over the years, he advanced in the ranks of the kingdom of darkness. In the video, he claims to hold degrees and certificates from schools of witchcraft in the UK, the USA and Mexico, one of them Hogwarts [sic] in the United States [sic]. He proudly repeats his title of Junior Grand Master of the Eastern, Southern and Central region of Africa several times. But, he shares, in the end, after being prayed over by many Christians for a long time, he was delivered from Satanism and became born again. The general thrust of this testimony is similar to other testimonies that have been collected by FENZA, or described in academic literature.

It is because of promised riches that Mr. Mulenga's mother became a Satanist. History repeated itself when Mr. Mulenga was seven years old:

> My mother wanted to have some money. So what she did was she consulted her mom, who was already into witchcraft. My grandma told my mother: If you want to have money, I'll show you the way to get it. . . . When I went to school I started admiring things. I said to myself: I want to be like my mom—but I didn't know where she was getting her riches from. She said: For me to have all those riches . . . what I did was I killed people, I sacrificed blood to the devil.

Satanism is portrayed as an alternative way to the promised land of modernity, with its possibilities for education, occupation and wealth. Mr. Mulenga had experienced difficulties in his education—"I even stopped going to school," he says—but as a Satanist he received degrees and certificates from all over the world. Many young people today struggle to find a paid job, but Mr. Mulenga had a position in the multinational organization of Satanism. He even advanced in position from Junior Assistant to Junior Grand Master. As a Satanist, he was part of a global network with all the commodities of an important job:

> He gave me a vehicle, he gave me a house, he gave me money. . . . I had my laptop—I was busy typing—and I had my phone, I was communicating to the agents of the devil somewhere.

Everything that modernity promised to bring is there in Satanism. This and other testimonies show the desire for prosperity and power in young men (and women): "They wanted to be strong, rich, influential and see the world (ideals that had earlier enticed young men to become Christians)" (Meyer 1999:203).

The promised land of modernity hasn't manifested itself in the ordinary world that Christians experience. And even in Satanism, the quest for prosperity comes at a price: Mr. Mulenga was told to sacrifice a family member if he wants to become a real Satanist. "Don't sacrifice me," his mother tells him, while they are living in Namibia. "Go to Zambia and sacrifice your father; I'll give you the address." The ties of family proved to be strong:

> When I came to my father's place, I discovered that my father was a man who had a heart for the children. He loved me so much, and I failed to kill him because of the love that he showed me. He was married again to another woman, who was my stepmother. She would mistreat me, she used to push me, do a lot of things. So I asked them: I cannot kill my father, but . . . Finally they said they wanted me to sacrifice my stepmother.

In this testimony, it is clear that to attain the riches of modernity, you have to sacrifice the bonds with your kin. The Lusaka-based Faith and Encounter Center (FENZA) has produced an informative documentary on Satanism. In this film actors re-enact experiences of Satanism that were collected by the FENZA group Fingers of Thomas. Sacrificing family members (and how difficult that is) is an important theme here as well (Udelhoven 2010).

According to the academic literature on Satanic confessions, the testimony is a place to enact the troubling sides of modernity (cf. Meyer 1999 and Frankfurter 2006). I believe that the discourse on Satanism does more than that. Satanism is not just the place where dreams of modernity come true and where ambiguous experiences can be voiced; it also offers an explanation for the flaws of contemporary modernity. People are still poor, fall ill and die. Roads—the infrastructure that promised to bring prosperity to all—claim many victims in accidents. In Mr. Mulenga's testimony these flaws are explained as a Satanic conspiracy:

> I can steal somebody's face and impersonate him. Going to the hospital I become like the doctor. Then I would get a syringe and go from bed to bed injecting people. At the end of the day 30 people could die at the same time in the hospital. The doctors couldn't

> even understand why these people have died. They would say: But the doctor was just here—not knowing that it me. We also used to cause accidents, using the force of darkness. We would cast a spell on the driver and he would just break out, and the vehicle would turn and the people would die.

Hospitals, infrastructure, education: these were supposed to bring the dreamed-for modernity to Zambia, but people experience flaws in these institutions. In their testimonies, ex-Satanists give an explanation for the shortcomings of contemporary modernity and in that a way to deal with experiences of disappointment.

Contemporary Zambia, with its—what scholars would call—modernity, is a source of inequality and exploitation in the experience of ordinary Zambians. These "nightmares" of modernity are mirrored in the Satanic world:

> My mother would send some men to come at night and she would use the knife to hurt them. She used to sell their hearts in Durban at the sea, where they use it to lure the sharks. You know they believe there are some minerals in the shark, and they need the heart of a human being.

To extract minerals, people are being exploited—Comaroff and Comaroff speak of "occult economies" in this sense: "a macabre, visceral economy founded on the violence of extraction and abstraction," where occult forces are used for cheap labor and body parts make a quick profit (1999:293).

Mr. Mulenga's turn to Christianity starts with a dream in which a man enters his room and asks him to look at himself. Doing so, he sees chains all over his body. "I asked him: Are you the one that has bound me like this? He said: No, I am not the one who has bound you, you have bound yourself." The man then introduces himself as "the Alpha and the Omega"—a phrase which Mr. Mulenga does not recognize at the time. Later on, when he has already accepted Christ in his life, Mr. Mulenga is involved in an accident. The story of what happens afterwards has a strong resemblance to this earlier dream:

> I started praying. I said: Father, is it your will for me to be in hospital? And God answered me to say: It is not my will. Now, I had bandages all over my body, and I started untying those bandages. I threw them away and I started walking.

It is only after he unties his former bonds that Mr. Mulenga is able to become a true Christian and start preaching about his experiences.

Testimonies like Mr. Mulenga's enact the dreams of modernity. They remind the audience of what modernity promised to bring: money, jobs, education, health care, etc. At the same time these testimonies give an explanation for the ambiguities and flaws of contemporary modernity that many people experience today. According to the local discourse, modernity and Christianity go hand-in-hand. The testimonies show that—even if Satanism may bring the riches associated with modernity—Christianity is a stronger force that conquers. These testimonies give hope for a better future in which all Satanists will be delivered like Mr. Mulenga and the promised land of modernity will become a truly Christian country.

Conclusion

Zambians dream of a promised land of modernity, in which there is health and wealth for everyone. In the local discourse, modernity is closely linked to the Christian faith. In reality, the dreams of modernity have not materialized: Zambia is still a poor country, stricken hard by the HIV/AIDS epidemic. This induces a climate of disappointment in the historical mission churches and suspicion against the happy few that have prospered.

Testimonies of involvement with Satanism give Christian congregations a safe place to dream of the spoils of modernity: riches, education and a job in an international organization. Also, I suggest that the testimony of a Satanic conspiracy gives an explanation of the flaws and ambiguities of modernity. If the health and wealth of modernity have not materialized, it is because of this strong kingdom of darkness. In the end the powers of the good are victorious: the Satanist repents, is delivered and becomes born again.

I asked in the introduction to this article whether it is a coincidence that testimonies of involvement in Satanism are particularly popular in Pentecostal churches, with their emphasis on prosperity. I think it is not a coincidence. In the mission churches modernity and Christianity were traditionally linked together, but this package deal hasn't manifested itself in the experience of many Christians. The prosperity gospel in Pentecostal churches offers a reconciliation between Christianity and the promised land of modernity: it gives congregants the opportunity to dream of attaining

Part 4: CULTURAL ANALYSIS

health and wealth in a Christian setting, a setting in which the temptation of using evil means to become prosperous is overcome.

Bibliography

Ashforth, A. 1996. "Of Secrecy and the Commonplace: Witchcraft and Power in Soweto." *Social Research* 63, no. 4:1183–1234.

Bastian, M. L. 2001. "Vulture Men, Campus Cultists and Teenaged Witches: Modern Magics in Nigerian Popular Media." In H. L. Moore and T. Sanders, eds., *Magical Interpretations, Material Realities: Modernity, Witchcraft and the Occult in Postcolonial Africa*, 71–96. London: Routledge.

Behrend, H. 2007. "The Rise of Occult Powers, AIDS and the Roman Catholic Church in Western Uganda." *Journal of Religion in Africa* 37:41–58.

Bruce, S. 2002. *God Is Dead: Secularization in the West*. Oxford: Blackwell Publishing.

Comaroff, J., and J. L. Comaroff, eds. 1993. *Modernity and Its Malcontents: Ritual and Power in Postcolonial Africa*. Chicago: University of Chicago Press.

———. 1999. "Occult Economies and the Violence of Abstraction: Notes from the South African Postcolony." *American Ethnologist* 26, no. 2:279–303.

Dobbelaere, K. 2009. "The Meaning and Scope of Secularization." In P. B. Clarke, ed., *The Oxford Handbook of the Sociology of Religion*, 599–615. Oxford: Oxford University Press.

Ellis, S. 2011. *Het regenseizoen: Afrika in de wereld*. Amsterdam: Bert Bakker.

Evans-Pritchard, E. E. 2010 [1937]. "Men Bewitch Others When They Hate Them." In D. Hicks, ed., *Ritual and Belief: Readings in the Anthropology of Religion*, 244–52. Lanham: Altamira Press.

Fardon, R., W. Van Binsbergen, and R. Van Dijk, eds. 1999. *Modernity on a Shoestring: Dimensions of Globalization, Consumption and Development in Africa and Beyond*. Leiden: EIDOS.

Ferguson, J. 1999. *Expectations of Modernity: Myths and Meanings of Urban Life on the Zambian Copperbelt*. Berkeley: University of California Press.

Frankfurter, D. 2006. *Evil Incarnate: Rumors of Demonic Conspiracy and Satanic Abuse in History*. Princeton: Princeton University Press.

Geschiere, P. 1997. *The Modernity of Witchcraft: Politics and the Occult in Postcolonial Africa*. Charlottesville: University of Virginia Press.

Giddens, A., and C. Pierson. 1998. *Conversations with Anthony Giddens: Making Sense of Modernity*. Stanford: Stanford University Press.

Heelas, P., and L. Woodhead. 2005. *The Spiritual Revolution: Why Religion Is Giving Way to Spirituality*. Oxford: Blackwell Publishing.

Meyer, B. 1999. *Translating the Devil: Religion and Modernity among the Ewe in Ghana*. London: Edinburgh University Press.

Meyer, B., and P. Pels, eds. 2003. *Magic and Modernity: Interfaces of Revelation and Concealment*. Stanford: Stanford University Press.

Moore, H. L., and T. Sanders, eds. 2001. *Magical Interpretations, Material Realities: Modernity, Witchcraft and the Occult in Postcolonial Africa*. London: Routledge.

Moore, S. F. 1999. "Reflections on the Comaroff Lecture." *American Ethnologist* 26, no. 2:304–6.

Oldridge, D. 2012. *The Devil: A Very Short Introduction*. Oxford: Oxford University Press.
Stark, R. 1999. "Secularization, R.I.P." *Sociology of Religion* 60:249–73.
Stolz, F. 1997. *Grundzüge der Religionswissenschaft*. 2nd ed. Göttingen: Vandenhoeck & Ruprecht.
Thompson, J. B. 1996. "Tradition and Self in a Mediated World." In P. Heelas, S. Lash, and P. Morris, eds., *Detraditionalization*, 89–108. Cambridge: Blackwell Publishing.
Tranberg Hansen, K. 1999. "Second-Hand Clothing Encounters in Zambia: Global Discourses, Western Commodities and Local Histories." In R. Fardon, W. Van Binsbergen, and R. Van Dijk, eds., *Modernity on a Shoestring: Dimensions of Globalization, Consumption and Development in Africa and Beyond*, 207–26. Leiden: EIDOS.
Udelhoven, B. 2008. "Satanism in Zambia: A New Tree with Old Roots." *FENZA* [online]. Available at: http://www.fenza.org/documents.html.
———. 2009a. "Cases of Satanism: Touched by the 'Fingers of Thomas.'" *FENZA* [online]. Available at: http://www.fenza.org/documents.html.
———. 2009b. "The Social Side of Possession (in Zambian Satanism)." *FENZA* [online]. Available at: http://www.fenza.org/documents.html.
———. 2009c. "Satanism and the Gospel of Prosperity." *FENZA* [online]. Available at: http://www.fenza.org/documents.html.
———. 2010. *Satanism—An Eye-Witness Account*. FENZA [film, online]. Available at: http://www.fenza.org/film-satanism.html.
World Databank. 2012. "World Development Indicators and Global Development Finance." World Bank [online]. Available at: http://databank.worldbank.org.

Primary Sources

Reader's comment. 2012. "Riots Break Out in Chambisi." Zambian Watchdog [online], 1 September 2012. Available at: http://www.zambianwatchdog.com/?p=41115&cpage=1#comments.
Testimonies of Heaven and Hell. 2011. "Ex-Satanist Gideon Mulenga—Set Free By Jesus!" Testimonies of Heaven and Hell [online]. Available at: http://www.testimoniesofheavenandhell.com/2011/03/ex-satanist-gideon-mulenga-set-free-by-jesus/.

9

African Gospreneurship

Assessing the Possible Contribution of the Gospel of Prosperity to Entrepreneurship in Light of Jesus's Teaching on Earthly Possessions

LOVEMORE TOGARASEI

THE PROSPERITY GOSPEL[1] HAS received its fair share of criticism. Authority on the New Testament Prof. S. McKnight (2009), for example, argues strongly against this gospel, saying the gospel makes God a vending machine into which believers put in faith, and get out blessings—"money, homes, cars, beautiful spouses, clever kids, good neighbors, big churches, and plush vacations." Referring to several biblical personalities, from Abraham to Paul, who obeyed God but lived no lives of prosperity, McKnight describes the prosperity gospel as "hogwash." He says Christian life is characterized by carrying the cross as Jesus taught, with God's expectation from the believers being that they need to trust and be faithful to him

---

1. What I call the prosperity gospel here is known by many other terms. "Positive confession," "faith gospel," "name it and own it," "health and wealth" are some of the terms used to describe it. In short, this is the teaching that God has already granted believers all they need through the death of Jesus; therefore all that the believer has to do is to believe and he/she will have God's blessings in wealth and health.

in blessings or in suffering. This attitude towards the prosperity gospel is widespread. For example, D. Jones (1998) takes a similar position against the prosperity gospel. He isolates and examines four crucial areas of error relating to the prosperity gospel's teachings: the Abrahamic covenant, atonement, giving and faith. Jones then exposes the erroneous ways in which these doctrines are presented in Pentecostal teaching. Another criticism of this gospel is given by H. T. Kroesbergen who writes in this publication, "There are at least two ways in which I fail to understand the prosperity gospel. On the one hand the message of the prosperity gospel with its emphasis on this-worldly goods, seems to me to be completely at odds with Christianity: biblically, historically and theologically. On the other hand the message of the prosperity gospel seems to me to be simply factually not true. [. . .] I am tempted to say that the prosperity gospel is simply unchristian and foolish."

The prosperity gospel is also criticized for its individualism and its this-worldly theology.[2] In a forthcoming book chapter, M. R. Gunda cites a Zimbabwean newspaper columnist who refers to the prosperity gospel as "anti-Christ voodoo capitalism." For a biblical scholar like me, the debate on the Christianness or otherwise of this doctrine is interesting for many reasons, chief of which is how the Bible is used in the acceptance or rejection of the doctrine. It can be observed from several prosperity gospel discourses[3] and Pentecostal scholars' writings (e.g., Gifford 2008), that the Pentecostal prosperity gospel has the Old Testament as its source book. The wealth of such men as Abraham and the other patriarchs is used as a sure promise that those who have faith in God, walk in God's ways in terms of tithing and observance of his statutes will be blessed by him in the here and now.

On the other hand, as we have seen in the case of McKnight, cited above, those who criticize this doctrine mainly base their arguments on New Testament teaching, particularly Jesus's teaching on material possessions and carrying our cross. It is often argued that Jesus (and Paul after

---

2. Although in its Western form prosperity gospel is said to promote individualism, this is not completely true in the African context. S. Hunt (2000:331–47) correctly concludes after analyzing several studies, "Therefore, faith teachings in the African churches and elsewhere are more likely to advance doctrines related to the community and the congregation, including prosperity and hard work, rather than to individual success." See also L. Togarasei (2006:114–32).

3. See, for example, M. R. Gunda and L. Togarasei (forthcoming) on Zimbabwean Pentecostal preachers' use of the Old Testament to support the gospel of prosperity.

him) emphasized a theology of the cross (*theologia crusis*) as opposed to a theology of glory (*theologia gloriae*). In the Zimbabwean public discourse, for example (Gunda, forthcoming), questions are asked on whether Jesus, the early Jerusalem community, Paul and the entire New Testament community taught and practiced such a gospel. What were their attitudes toward wealth? What were their attitudes toward poverty? This article has been prompted by such questions. Considering the centrality of Jesus in the Christian faith, the article seeks to analyze his teaching on the wealth. Finally, after establishing Jesus's position on earthly possessions, the article ends with an assessment of the possible contribution of the prosperity gospel to entrepreneurship.

Jesus's Attitude Toward Earthly Possessions

Any discussion of Jesus almost always faces the problem of the authentic Jesus material. Did Jesus say and do what the gospel writers say he said and did? What alterations or additions did the early church and the evangelists make to the sayings and deeds of Jesus? It is because of this that scholars have wrestled with the question of the historical Jesus throughout the period of critical biblical scholarship.[4] Fortunately for our discussion, Jesus's attitude to earthly possessions has been identified through the criteria of authenticity, as one of the authentic sayings of Jesus because of its radicalism. Our sources for his attitude are mainly the Synoptic Gospels.

Jesus lived in a society where, as in every society, people generally treasured being well-off. Judaism, as a religion, did not contrast between God and riches, between earthly possessions and heavenly possessions. Deutronomistic theology saw riches as a sign of blessing by God, whereas poverty was seen as a sign of God's curse.[5] As Braun (1979:81) correctly observes, the renunciation of earthly possessions was taught only in extreme cases: for instance, if someone dedicated his life completely to the study of the law. Into such a tradition Jesus appeared, with his own teaching on

---

4. I. du Plessis (1987:12–23) divides the history of New Testament scholarship on the historical Jesus into three phases. However, the debate has not ended (Dawes 1999).

5. See, for example, Deuteronomy 7:12–13, "And because you hearken to these ordinances, and keep and do them, the Lord your God will keep with you the covenant and the steadfast love which he swore to your fathers to keep, he will love you, bless you, and multiply you; he will also bless the fruit of your body and the fruit of your ground, your grain and your wine and your oil, the increase of your cattle and the young of your flock" (RSV).

the accumulation of riches. It is this teaching that can help us to establish Jesus's attitude to earthly possessions in the context of kingdom teaching. To establish this attitude we need to analyze the passages where Jesus talked about earthly possessions.

The Lukan version of the first beatitude can be an interesting starting point for our discussion. The Revised Standard Version (RSV) puts it thus: "Blessed are you poor, for yours is the kingdom of God" (Luke 6:20). Matthew's version of the beatitude is slightly different as he talks of "the poor in spirit" (Matt 5:3). There is a general consensus among exegetes, for example, Matura (1984:75) and Braun (1979:81), that the Lukan version is the authentic one as the Matthean one is treated as an attempt to soften the hard saying of Jesus. Furthermore, the Lukan beatitude is attested to in many other sayings of Jesus on earthly possessions, as we shall see below. It is also the form in which the beatitude is found in the Gospel of Thomas (Gospel of Thomas, Saying 54). The poor, in Luke, are both spiritually and materially poor, showing that here Jesus did not teach the prosperity gospel. As our analysis of other passages shows below, it would appear, from face value, that Jesus was against the accumulation of earthly possessions. This is the reading and interpretation that those who find the prosperity gospel to be unchristian would note.

The story of the rich young ruler is one often-cited story on Jesus's attitude towards earthly possessions. Apart from minor differences,[6] the story is told in almost the same way in the three synoptic gospels: Mark 10:17–31, Matthew 19: 16–30 and Luke 18:18–30. In all three a rich man asks Jesus what he should do to inherit eternal life. Jesus states six commandments, which the man says he has observed since his youth. Jesus then tells him to sell all his possessions, distribute the proceeds among the poor and follow him. Because of his many possessions, the rich man is sad and goes away. This incident is then followed by Jesus's teaching on how hard it is for rich people to obtain eternal life: "It is easier for a camel to go through the eye of a needle than for a rich man to enter the kingdom of God" (Mark 10:24). In Palestine, where the camel was the largest animal, and the eye of the needle, the smallest hole, the words of Jesus stressed the impossibility of the rich to enter eternal life. It is because of this radicalism that Matura (1984:69) says the following about the statement: "The unqualified, absolute declaration and the difficulty of applying and interpreting it clearly demonstrate that

---

6. For example, Matthew avoids Jesus's embarrassing declaration that only God is good.

Part 4: CULTURAL ANALYSIS

the saying was not created by a community but was transmitted as if coming from the Lord." Based on the criteria suggested to find the authentic Jesus's statements[7], this statement qualifies as one of the authentic sayings of Jesus because of its radicalism. It is hard to explain why the early church would have invented this radical saying and attributed it to Jesus. Now, if this statement is from Jesus, is the prosperity gospel justified?

We do not need to answer the above question at this point because there are many ways of interpreting the statement that riches and attainment of eternal life are incompatible.[8] It seems the camel-needle comparison was a common proverb. The Koran (7:38) has it and the Talmud (B. Berak. 55b) has elephant instead of camel but presents the same teaching (Hill 1972:284). Thus one way of looking at Jesus's statement would be simply to treat it as a proverb. However, what Jesus went on to say shows that he did not use the statement proverbially: "With men it is impossible, but not with God, for all things are possible with God" (Mark 10:27). What this means, then, is that anyone's salvation is a miracle since it is based on God's act. Thus, according to D. Hill (1972:284), what Jesus meant is, "The salvation of rich men, though beyond the ability of men, is within the power of God, who can inspire them with a new sense of values." Often the interpretation against the prosperity gospel is that Jesus shows that riches are spiritually dangerous and that earthly possessions and participation in the final salvation are mutually exclusive. The question, however, is whether Jesus was referring to this specific man and other specific situations, or whether he meant the teaching to be applied universally. A quick answer to the question would be that, from Mark 10:17–22 and the parallel passages, there is surely no indication that Jesus intended this teaching to be universal. Matthew even says the rich man was to sell his possessions in order to be perfect, not necessarily to inherit the kingdom as any ordinary Christian (Matt 19:21).[9] We therefore, cannot make a final conclusion on

---

7. Clive Marsh and Steve Moyise (2006) give a brief discussion of the criteria for authenticity. For an elaborate discussion of the criteria, see Norman Perrin and Dennis Duling (1982).

8. From time to time Christians have attempted to soften the statement by, for example, suggesting that the Greek word for "camel" means a ships cable, or that the "eye of the needle" indicates the opening in a gate (Braun 1979:81–82).

9. The word perfect (*teleios*) appears twice in the Synoptic Gospels, in both cases in Matthew (5:48 and 19:21). Our understanding of perfect here is that of a condition reserved for an exclusive class of people who decide to abandon "ordinary" life for a life dedicated only to the service of God. We would compare this to the lives of people who decide to become full-time priests/ministers. We therefore distinguish being "perfect"

Jesus's attitude towards earthly possessions on the basis of the story of the rich man. We need to further investigate other passages where Jesus talked about the same topic.

Apart from the long story of the rich man, the evangelists also recorded several sayings of Jesus showing his attitude to earthly possessions. The authenticity of these passages cannot be established with certainty but, guided by their radicalism, we can proceed to treat them here as authentic Jesus sayings. In Matthew 6:24/Luke 16:13, Jesus talks about how riches present an alternative god to those who love them: "You cannot serve God and Mammon." This is the only occasion where Jesus personified money to show its danger. He compared the power of material possessions to that of a divine being: money can be worshipped by those who love it in the same way God is worshipped. Thus, true treasure is heavenly, not earthly (Matt 6:19–21/Luke 12: 33–34). After all, Jesus taught that there is no need for one to be anxious or preoccupied with food and clothing, for the heavenly Father provides these (Matt 6:25/Luke 12:22–31).

The Gospel of Luke has by far the most abundant texts on material possessions. This abundance is attributed to the possibility that the community to which the author addressed his gospel was characterized by a general renunciation of possessions. Considering that, of all the instances he mentions, there is only one specific instance in which the renunciation of possessions turned out well—that of Barnabas of Cyprus (Acts 4:36)—there is no doubt that "we have before us the author's idealizing exaggeration of individual cases" (Braun 1979:85), possibly including the story of Barnabas. Besides these exaggerations we can get some insights from the author's opinion concerning Jesus's attitude to earthly possessions, particularly if this evidence corresponds with Jesus's general attitude. In Luke 12:13–34, we have Jesus invited to judge on a dispute pertaining to material possessions. Jesus refuses to be involved in such matters. Rather, he gives a parable which is meant to teach the futility of amassing material stores for the future (La Verdiere 1980:174). Through the parable he demonstrates that one's possessions do not guarantee one's life. In 16:19–31, Luke also tells us of Jesus's parable of the rich man and Lazarus. On earth the rich man, who "was dressed in purple and fine linen" enjoyed all his life, feasting every day. On the other hand, the poor man, Lazarus, scraped to get the

---

from being an ordinary Christian. We are aware, however, that there are exegetes like Matura (1984) and Hill (1972) who go against this interpretation. Our interpretation follows that of Braun (1979:83).

bare minimum for his life needs. As Matura (1984:89) says, "The only thing between the two is a gulf of indifference." However, upon their deaths, the situation reverses itself: Lazarus reclines with Abraham, while the rich man looks on in misery. The story echoes Jesus's words, "Woe to you who that are rich now, for you have received your consolation" (Luke 6:24). From these two parables, one gets an impression that, for Jesus, earthly possessions are incompatible with or at least a hindrance to the inheritance of the kingdom. As E. Earle Ellis (1974:205–6) notes from these parables, "(they) express the truth that one's status in life is reversed at death."

Our analysis above presents to us a Jesus who treated earthly possessions as a hindrance to the attainment of eternal life. From this analysis one can therefore find the Pentecostal prosperity gospel to be incompatible with the teaching of Jesus. However, there are many other sayings of Jesus that need to be considered before one draws a final conclusion. The evangelists show that Jesus had some rich followers. All the gospels occasionally reveal that some followers of Jesus had houses of their own. Peter (Mark 1:29 and the parallel passages), Levi (Mark 2:15 and the parallel passages) and Mary and Martha (Luke 10:38) serve as examples. There is also mention of well-to-do people among Jesus's friends and followers: the women who ministered to him out of their resources (Luke 8:3) and Joseph of Arimathea (Mark 15:43 and the parallel passages). Luke also tells us of Jesus's relationship with rich tax collectors like Zacchaeus (Luke 19:1–10). In all his dealings with these well-to-do people, we do not find Jesus asking them to renounce their earthly possessions. What then does this tell us of Jesus's attitude to earthly possessions?

We have argued, in the case of the rich man and other passages, that it appears Jesus did not intend to make the renunciation of earthly possessions universal and legalistic. Coupled with what we have just observed (that Jesus had well-to-do followers), this seems to show that Jesus did not consider earthly possessions to be evil. Rather, there appears to be more than what meets the eye in Jesus's denunciation and call for renunciation of earthly possessions. Our reading of Jesus's attitude from the sum total of his teaching and practice is that he did not reject the rich or riches, but rather he challenged the rich in radical ways to use their riches justifiably: for the good of all humanity. We now turn to demonstrate this using gospel records.

In the story of the rich young man, Jesus calls the rich man to sell his possessions and distribute the proceeds to the poor. The words of Jesus do not mean that possessions should be sold because they are evil. Rather, selling them is meant to achieve two things. First, in the case of this young man, it enables him to be able to follow Jesus. It appears Jesus called for the renunciation of earthly possessions only where they formed a stumbling block to discipleship. Thus the demand to the rich man to get rid of his possessions should be seen within the framework of Christian discipleship. Selling of possessions, as De Santa Ana (1979:27) says, shows a disciple's unconditional readiness to follow his master. In fact, Jesus did not just teach about the renunciation of earthly possessions, but also about the cutting of relationships: family life, including home, parents, brothers and sisters (Mark 10:28–29). Also, the selling of possessions is meant to assist the poor. The Greek term used for the poor is "*ptochos*" and includes all kinds of the underprivileged: the weak, the deprived, the helpless, the needy and so on. The proceeds from the selling of the rich man's possessions would be given as "alms" to the poor. The term "alms" is usually used to refer to a gift offered to the needy for love of God. De Santa Ana (1979:27) says such a gift generally has no profound effect on the life of the receiver but is understood as assistance which alleviates his condition without allowing him to overcome it.

Though earthly possessions are not evil, Jesus shows that they are dangerous. He describes them as "unrighteous mammon" (Luke 16:9–11), they are a source of anxiety and worry (Matt 6:25–34) and a deception (Mark 4:19), they enslave (Matt 6:24), and they also choke the Word (Mark 4:10) and prevent people from seeking the kingdom (Matt 6:33). Riches also provide false security (Luke 12:16–21).The evangelists, particularly Luke, show that, to escape from the threat posed by earthly possessions, Jesus advocated for their proper use. By giving alms, the Pharisees, who were lovers of money, could have made everything pure, even those possessions obtained from extortion and wickedness (Luke 11:41). Zacchaeus, who had defrauded people, was commended for giving a four times restitution (Luke 19:1–10). Jesus, therefore, insisted on generosity with one's possessions. One must give abundantly, even (Luke 6:30), not expecting anything in return (Luke 6:34–35)— what one social scientist, M. D. Sahlins (1974) has called generalized "reciprocity." The right use of earthly possessions for Jesus, therefore, is charity. Those who have left everything for the sake of discipleship will receive a hundredfold (Mark 10:30) and those who give to the poor will receive an overflowing measure (Luke 6:38).

Part 4: CULTURAL ANALYSIS

But by calling the rich to share their possessions with the poor, was Jesus advocating for a life of poverty? The answer to this question can also help us analyse the Pentecostal prosperity gospel. Matura (1984:99) provides us with an answer to the question. He writes, "Paradoxically, even Luke, called 'the evangelist of the poor,' speaks more about material possessions, their danger and their usage, than about the poor and poverty." The fact that Jesus had well-to-do disciples also shows that he did not advocate for poverty. He did not ignore the fact that man's material needs must be met. In the first temptation story, Jesus answered the devil, "Man shall not live by bread alone" (Matt 4:4/Luke 4:4). Inversely, this statement also means that man cannot live without bread. Even in the prayer that he taught his disciples, he taught them to pray, "Give us this day our daily bread" (Matt 6:11/Luke 11:3). Thus Jesus implied that humanity needs daily provisions, not poverty. Therefore, the road that Jesus was proposing for the rich was not that of poverty, "but that of charity implicit in the duty of almsgiving" (de Santa Ana 1972:33).

Overall, our analysis of the Gospels, therefore, shows that Jesus did not consider earthly possessions to be evil. He, however, considered them dangerous if not used properly for the benefit of the poor. The proper use of earthly possessions, for him, should take the form of charity towards the poor. From this position of Jesus, what then can we say about the Pentecostal prosperity gospel? Is it justifiable to condemn it on the argument that it contradicts Jesus's teaching?

Analysis of the Pentecostal Gospel in Light of Jesus's Attitude to Earthly Possessions

Except for a few Pentecostal preachers,[10] most do not use Jesus to support the prosperity gospel. As mentioned above, their source book is the Old Testament. However, Jesus did not promote poverty among his followers. He provided the hungry with food, showing that a believer must have enough for himself. As we have seen, Jesus taught his disciples to pray for

10. For example, Andrew Wutawunashe of the Family of God Church in Zimbabwe uses Matthew 9:37 ("The harvest is truly plenteous but the labourers are few") for prosperity. Andrew sees all FOG members as being called in this passage to be labourers in the field. They are to harvest souls, money, material things (e.g. cars, houses), influence and power. Also, in interpreting John 4:35 ("Lift up your eyes and look on the fields, for they are white, ready to harvest"), he again talks of the Christian's need to see what to collect here on earth: health, holiness, power, money and material things (Togarasei 2005a).

enough bread for the day. He also did not advocate poverty, and, if we accept the gospel of John, Jesus and his disciples had a fund to keep them going and to assist the poor (John 12:6). Perhaps the criticism of the prosperity gospel by those we have cited above and those of like-mindedness indicates that they are not aware of what prosperity means, especially in the African context. Elsewhere (Togarasei 2011) I argue that the prosperity gospel can help with poverty alleviation in Africa. This is because, among many Africans, prosperity means having food on the table and affording the basic life needs: sending children to school, buying clothes, having a car that takes you from one point to another or even affording the public transport fares.

Indeed, affording the above basic necessities is what African Pentecostals consider as a sign of God's blessing. Pentecostals see the poor as possessed by a spirit of poverty that needs to be cast out. This may seem to be against Jesus's blessing of the poor, but when one understands what poverty really means in Africa (malnourished babies, plastic houses, food cooked using plastic paper for fuel, an entire family sharing one blanket) surely no one can consider these to be the blessings of God. As Pentecostals say, such poverty is indeed a hindrance to the true worship of God. Thus, one draw card for Pentecostals is their promise of wealth (in actual fact, dignified life, for at least some African Pentecostals) to those who accept Jesus. For such people, Pentecostalism "is the only way people can be connected to the modern world of commodities, media and financial flows" (Marshal-Fratani 1998:282–96). What African Pentecostalism thereby endeavors to do is also to modernize Africans. There is, therefore, a clear connection between Pentecostalism and modernity. Thus, looking to developed Western countries where life is obviously better than in many parts of Africa, for African Pentecostals contact with London, New York, Paris and other Western cities is a mark of progress and a sign of God's blessing. Many, therefore, have opened church branches in these Western cities and/or have invited speakers from these countries to come and preach at their conventions. This connects African Pentecostals and those from the developed world. Poverty is linked to African traditional "things" while "growth in Christ" or "blessings" is seen in flashy cars, successful careers and riches in general. No wonder the consumers of this gospel are generally those who are well-to-do.[11]

---

11. There are also many poor people in these churches. However, these are given hope by the gospel preached and always see themselves as on an upward journey to success.

Notwithstanding the above, there are, however, areas where the Pentecostal gospel seems to clash with the teaching of Jesus. The claim that all Pentecostals should have cars and houses finds no trace in Jesus's teaching and practice. Rather, according to Matthew and Luke, Jesus, though being the Son of God, was worse off than foxes and birds which have holes and nests respectively. He had "nowhere to lay his head" (Matt 8:20/Luke 9:58). Though some of his disciples had houses, as we have seen above, Jesus never taught that that was a sign of God's blessing. Instead he taught that, for the sake of discipleship, sometimes property was a hindrance.

Some Pentecostal claims that God can miraculously credit your bank account[12] also appear farfetched. Another discontinuity between Jesus's and the Pentecostal attitude to earthly possessions is seen in their approaches to the use of possessions. As we have seen, for Jesus the best use of earthly possessions is for solidarity with the poor and the exploited. This is different from the attitude in some Pentecostal churches, where riches seem to be for individual social mobility. Each born-again strives to achieve the best for him/herself in life. As one Pentecostal once said, "God wants his children to live in the best houses, to worship him in the best buildings, to drive the best cars and even when they die to receive the best burials by the best funeral companies."[13] In such churches members are asked to give various kinds of offerings, but such offerings are used for the expansion of the churches and the upkeep of the pastors. Initially most African Pentecostal churches rarely participated in programs meant to uplift the lives of the poor in the communities they operate. As a result, they were accused of lacking "strong social consciences" (Togarasei 2005a:3–20).[14]

Gospreneurship: Prosperity Gospel and Entrepreneurship

I am indebted to my former student and now academic colleague, Masiiwa Ragies Gunda, who spotted this term—gospreneurship—in a Zimbabwean newspaper article critiquing the prosperity gospel. In that article, the author

12. This author heard such teachings from Uebert Angel of Spirit Embassy headquartered in Harare, Zimbabwe, University of Botswana Stadium, 26 October 2012.

13. Pastor M. Chinoda of the Family of God Church, interview, Harare, 14 July 2003.

14. This observation is reached on the basis of comparison of what Pentecostal and traditional mainline churches are doing in their respective societies. Indeed there are some Pentecostal churches involved in charity work, but, by and large, many of them are not (cf. Togarasei 2005b).

uses the term derogatively to refer to Pentecostal preachers' amassing of wealth for themselves through encouraging their followers to give in order to be blessed by God. Thus, the prosperity gospel becomes some form of entrepreneurship for these pastors. I, however, use the word differently in this article, as I am referring to possible contributions of the prosperity gospel to entrepreneurship. It is a truism that many African countries are experiencing severe rates of unemployment. Acknowledging that data for employment rates is difficult to come by in Africa, Africapedia gives the following rates (Zambia is not mentioned on this website):

Rank	Country	Unemployment rate	Year of data
1	Zimbabwe	95.00	2009
2	Djibouti	59.00	2007
3	Namibia	51.20	2008
4	Senegal	48.00	2007
5	Kenya	40.00	2008
6	Swaziland	40.00	2006
7	Mauritania	30.00	2008
8	South Africa	23.30	2010
9	Gabon	21.00	2006
10	Tunisia	14.00	2010

My argument is that it is therefore not a coincidence that the prosperity gospel has found fertile ground in most of these countries. This is because Pentecostal churches teach the need for one to create his/her employment. They therefore teach their followers entrepreneurship skills for survival, in order to prove the prosperity gospel true. Although I have listened to many Pentecostal sermons on this topic, I will devote space here to one given by Dr. Enock Sitima of Bible Life Ministries in Gaborone, Botswana, on 28 March 2010. I need to mention, however, that Dr. Sitima is a very good entrepreneurship motivator and this is only one of many such sermons I have heard him teach. On this particular day he opened the sermon by underlining that he teaches believers what schools and universities fail to do. He said African schools and universities prepare people for bondage. Instead of education, he said, what Africans need is an entrepreneurial spirit. He said this is what Pentecostalism teaches. For him, Pentecostalism helps believers to discover the operative for wealth creation and financial intelligence.

Part 4: CULTURAL ANALYSIS

In the sermon, Sitima attributed poverty in Africa to four causes, which he identified as nomadic mentality, consumer mentality, civil servant and salary mentality and materialism mentality. He defined nomadic mentality as the inability to focus on one thing, resulting in one losing direction in life. Consumer mentality was defined as the spirit of always spending what one has instead of thinking about investment. In line with the general Pentecostal discouragement of employment, civil servant and salary mentality was defined as the spirit of seeking employment instead of creating employment. The preacher emphasized that God never intended his followers to be employed but to be employers. In his own words, he said, "God never intended you to earn a salary but to earn an income." The audience was urged to confess, "God deliver me from salary mentality." The sermon ended with prayers for those who wanted to be delivered from the different poverty-causing mentalities. The whole teaching resonates with the spirit of capitalism. In fact, Sitima teaches that believers must learn to run businesses that can make money "even when you are asleep on holiday." No doubt, the prosperity gospel has been associated with the Western economic free market (Hunt 2006:331–47). For this reason some people have criticized it and even see it as collaborating with the powers that keep Africa poor and thereby contributing to poverty in Africa (Togarasei 2006:120). Although this can be true to some extent, it cannot be denied that entrepreneurship is one way to promote sustainable development in contexts where unemployment is rampant. Thus, the teachings on entrepreneurship by prosperity preachers should be welcomed.

Entrepreneurship teachings have led a sizeable number of Pentecostals to start their own businesses, thus contributing to poverty alleviation through employment creation. Some of the richest citizens of Botswana and Zimbabwe I know belong to Pentecostal churches. In Zimbabwe, for example, Pentecostal churches like Celebration Church boast of business moguls such as Strive Masiyiwa of Econet Wireless,[15] Nigel Chanakira of Kingdom Holdings[16] and leading medical doctors like Matthew Wazara. Members are found in farming, in education, in banking, in law, in transport and other such sectors. To encourage entrepreneurship, leading Pentecostal churches have business fellowships for men. In Zimbabwe, ZAOGA has the Africa Christian Business Fellowship, Family of God Church has

---

15. Econet Wireless is the largest Zimbabwean mobile telephone services provider.

16. Kingdom Holdings owns Kingdom Bank of Zimbabwe and Kingdom Bank Africa Ltd in other African countries like Botswana.

the Mighty Men's Project and Investments Desk and Celebration Church has the Victory Business Forum. All these groups help men with ideas for running their families and businesses. They lend members money to start their own projects. The women are also taught how to run income generation projects like poultry, candle-making and so on. Biblical figures are used to support the entrepreneurial spirit. Like Abraham, the born-agains are urged to be farmers and transport operators. Like the virtuous woman in Proverbs 31, they are urged to be cross-border traders. E. Dorier-Apprill (2001:301) also noted the Pentecostal entrepreneurial spirit in Brazzaville, Congo. She writes, "They reassert the value of individual initiative in the production of wealth, founding on the letter of the Bible the necessity of work and the entrepreneurial spirit. In this spirit the creation of business is no longer a last resort imposed by the crisis, but a true behavioral ethic founded on an ethic of belief." Pentecostal entrepreneurship is also found in the area of television and other media technologies (Paype 2009, Togarasei 2012). Thus the Pentecostal prosperity gospel is, for sure, encouraging entrepreneurship among many Africans faced by high rates of employment. With its teaching that God wants his children to live successful lives, Pentecostalism gives many Africans a positive mindset that they can make it in business through God, rather than by waiting for a Western donor to extend a helping hand. At this point in time perhaps much has not yet been achieved, but success stories of the indentified individuals above are encouraging signs. The old criticism of Pentecostals lacking a social conscience cannot be said today of such Pentecostal churches as the Zimbabwe Assemblies of God Africa/Forward in Faith International (ZAOGA/FIF), which is not only running hospitals, schools, and a television station, but is also in the process of establishing the first Pentecostal church-run university in Zimbabwe. According to Biri and Togarasei (forthcoming), this is thanks to the funds donated by its entrepreneur membership.[17]

---

17. Entrepreneurship in ZAOGA/FIF is taught through the doctrine of talents. Maxwell (2006:202) defines this doctrine following Martin as "penny capitalism," the vending of cheap food stuffs and clothes to finance the activities of the church. Although this definition is true of the beginnings of this practice, today "working talents" involves any other entrepreneurial activities outside one's main source of money. The practice is meant to make sure members are self sufficient.

Part 4: CULTURAL ANALYSIS

Conclusion

The Pentecostal prosperity gospel attracts debates among both scholars and ordinary Christians. In this article, I have approached the debate by focusing on those who dismiss the gospel on the basis that Jesus taught the need to carry one's cross. The article has analyzed Jesus's teaching on earthly/material possessions, concluding that, although Jesus did not teach the prosperity gospel, he also never celebrated poverty. There is no indication in his teaching that those who worship him must strive for more than the basic necessities of life. Thus, the Pentecostal prosperity gospel must encourage hard work for the sake of self-sustenance, not of greed. I therefore have argued that in African contexts of severe unemployment, the Pentecostal encouragement of entrepreneurship should surely be welcome. Perhaps the mistake in some prosperity preachers is to equate prosperity with spirituality. These are indeed different, but that should not mean that poverty equates spirituality. It has also been highlighted in this article that although they talk about prosperity, what many African prosperity preachers refer to is merely a life of dignity characterized by one affording the basic necessities of life. I would conclude that the missionary period of a pie-in-the-sky or wealth-in-heaven theology (which the missionaries themselves did not live but promoted among Africans), is surely no longer acceptable in postcolonial Africa.

Bibliography

Africapedia. 2011. "Unemployment Rates in Various African Countries." Africapedia [online]. Available at: http://www.africapedia.com/UNEMPLOYMENT-RATES-IN-VARIOUS-AFRICAN-COUNTRIES. Original source: https://www.cia.gov/library/publications/the-world factbook/rankorder/2129rank.html (currently not available).

Biri, K., and L. Togarasei. Forthcoming. "Pentecostal Churches: Money Making Machines or Purveyors of Socio-economic Growth?" In L. Togarasei, ed., *Spirit Filled: Pentecostal Christianity in Zimbabwe*.

Braun, H. 1979. *Jesus of Nazareth: The Man and His Times*. Philadelphia: Fortress Press.

Dawes, G. W., ed. 1999. *The Historical Jesus Quest: Landmarks in the Search for the Jesus of History*. Louisville, KY: Westminster John Knox Press.

De Santa Ana, J. 1979. *Good News to the Poor: The Challenge of the Poor in the History of the Church*. Maryknoll, NY: Orbis Books.

Dorier-Apprill, E. 2001. "The New Pentecostal Networks of Brazaville." In A. Corten and R. Marshal-Fratani, eds., *Between Babel to Pentecost: Transnational Pentecostalism in Africa and Latin America*, 293–308. London: Hurst and Company.

du Plessis, I. 1987. *Nazareth or Egypt: Who Was Right? A Historical Perspective on the New Testament*. Pretoria: J. L. van Schaik.
Earle Ellis, E. 1974. *The Gospel of Luke*. London: Marshall, Morgan and Scott.
Gifford, P. 2008. "Trajectories in African Christianity." *International Journal for the Study of the Christian Church* 8, no. 4:275–89.
Gunda, M. R. Forthcoming. "Pentecostal Gospel of Prosperity in Zimbabwe: Understanding the Divisive Nature of Mega-church Superstar Men of God (Prophets)." In L. Togarasei, ed., *Spirit Filled: Pentecostal Christianity in Zimbabwe*.
Gunda, M. R., and L. Togarasei, L. Forthcoming. "The Old Testament as a Source Book for the Pentecostal Gospel of Prosperity." In L. Togarasei, ed., *Spirit Filled: Pentecostal Christianity in Zimbabwe*.
Hill, D. 1972. *The Gospel of Matthew*. London: Marshal, Morgan and Scott.
Hunt, S. 2000. "'Winning Ways': Globalisation and the Impact of the Health and Wealth Gospel." *Journal of Contemporary Religion* 15, no. 3:331–47.
Jones, D. W. 1998. "The Bankruptcy of the Prosperity Gospel: An Exercise in Biblical and Theological Ethics." Bible.org [online]. Available at: http://bible.org/article/bankruptcy-prosperity-gospel-exercise-biblical-and-theological-ethics.
La Verdiere, E. 1980. *Luke*. Collegeville, MN: The Liturgical Press.
Marsh, C., and S. Moyise. 2006. *Jesus and the Gospels*. London: T&T Clark International.
Marshall-Fratani, R. 1998. "Mediating the Global and Local in Nigerian Pentecostalism." *Journal of Religion in Africa* 28, no. 3:282–96.
Matura, T. 1984. *Gospel Radicalism: The Hard Sayings of Jesus*. Maryknoll: Orbis Books.
Maxwell, D. 2006. *African Gifts of the Spirit: Pentecostalism and the Rise of a Zimbabwean Transnational Religious Movement*. Harare: Weaver Press.
McKnight, S. 2009. "The Problem for the Prosperity Gospel." Beliefnet [online]. Available at: http://www.beliefnet.com/Faiths/Christianity/2009/03/The-Problem-for-the-Prosperity-Gospel.aspx?p=1.
Paype, K. 2009. "'We Need to Open Up the Country': Development and the Christian Key Scenario in the Social Space of Kinshasa's Teleserials." *Journal of African Media Studies* 1, no. 1:101–16.
Perrin, N., and D. C. Duling. 1982. *The New Testament: An Introduction: Proclamation and Parenesis, Myth and History*. New York: Harcourt, Brace Jovanovich.
Sahlins, M. D. 1974. *Stone Age Economics*. London: Tavistock Publications Ltd.
Togarasei, L. 2005a. "Modern Pentecostalism as an Urban Phenomenon: The Case of the Family of God Church in Zimbabwe." *Exchange: Journal of Missiological and Ecumenical Research* 34, no. 4:349–75.
———. 2005b. "HIV/AIDS and the Role of the Church in Zimbabwe." *Africa Theological Journal* 28, no. 1:3–20.
———. 2006. "Cursed Be the Past: Tradition and Modernity among Modern Pentecostals in Zimbabwe and Botswana." *BOLESWA Journal of Theology, Religion and Philosophy* 1, no. 2:114–32.
———. "The Pentecostal Gospel of Prosperity in African Contexts of Poverty." *Exchange* 40:336–50.
———. 2012. "Mediating the Gospel: Pentecostal Christianity and Media Technology in Botswana and Zimbabwe." *Journal of Contemporary Religion* 27, no. 2:257–74.

List of Authors

Devison Telen Banda is lecturer in New Testament, Greek and hermeneutics at Justo Mwale Theological University College. From 2000 until 2009 he was principal of the institution. He holds a PhD in New Testament interpretation from the University of the Free State in South Africa. His research areas are the Pauline writings and the relationship between New Testament interpretation and African culture. He is a minister in the Reformed Church in Zambia.

Lameck Banda is lecturer in systematic theology at Justo Mwale Theological University College. He holds a PhD in systematic theology from the University of the Free State in South Africa. The title of his PhD project was "Hope in Suffering: An African Interpretation of Jesus's Resurrection." He is a minister in the Reformed Church in Zambia.

Victor Chilenje is lecturer in church history, missiology and ecclesiology at Justo Mwale Theological University College. He holds a PhD in church history from the University of Stellenbosch in South Africa. He researched the history of his own church, the Church of Central Africa, Presbyterian. He is a minister in this church, and the current Synod Projects Coordinator of the CCAP, Synod of Zambia.

Dustin W. Ellington is lecturer in New Testament and Greek at Justo Mwale Theological University College. He holds a PhD in New Testament Interpretation from Duke University in the USA. His research focus is on Paul's letters to the Corinthians, and Christian life and ministry in the New Testament. He is a minister in the Presbyterian Church (USA) and the Uniting Presbyterian Church in Southern Africa.

Johanneke Kroesbergen-Kamps is lecturer in religious studies, humanities and research methods at Justo Mwale Theological University College. She

List of Authors

holds an MA in religious studies from the Rijksuniversiteit Groningen, the Netherlands. Currently she is working on a PhD project in anthropology of religion that focuses on the relationship between confessions of former Satanists in Zambia and the arrival of modernity. She is a missionary on behalf of Kerk in Actie, the mission department of the Protestant Church in the Netherlands.

Hermen Kroesbergen is lecturer in systematic theology, ethics and philosophy of religion at Justo Mwale Theological University College and postdoctoral fellow at the University of Pretoria. He holds a PhD in systematic theology from the Protestant Theological University in the Netherlands. His research focuses on the interpretation of ordinary language of faith. He is a minister in the Protestant Church in the Netherlands and the Reformed Church in Zambia.

Lukas R. K. Soko is lecturer in practical theology at Justo Mwale Theological University College. He holds a PhD in practical theology from the University of Stellenbosch in South Africa. He researched schisms and church leadership in his own church, the Reformed Church in Zambia. He is a minister in this church.

Lovemore Togarasei is professor in the department of Theology and Religious Studies at the University of Botswana. He teaches courses in biblical studies, Greek and new religious movements. He holds a PhD in New Testament studies/African Christianity from the University of Zimbabwe. His research focus is on biblical studies and African Christianity.

Edwin Zulu is lecturer in Old Testament and Hebrew at Justo Mwale Theological University College and research associate of the department of Old and New Testament at Stellenbosch University. He holds a PhD in Old Testament from Stellenbosch University in South Africa. His research areas include Bible and context, narrative literature, Ruth, and biblical interpretation. He is a minister in the Reformed Church in Zambia, and the current moderator of this church.

www.ingramcontent.com/pod-product-compliance
Lightning Source LLC
Chambersburg PA
CBHW071444160426
43195CB00013B/2026